About the TLS

The *Times Literary Supplement* was born in January 1902. Its first ever front page bashfully stated that 'during the Parliamentary session Literary Supplements to "The Times" will appear as often as may be necessary in order to keep abreast with the more important publications of the day'. Fortunately, the question of necessity was not left in the hands of literary journalists (who, we can imagine, might occasionally push for a holiday or two), and the title became a weekly one. A few years later, the *TLS* split entirely from *The Times*.

Since then, we have prided ourselves on being the world's leading magazine for culture and ideas. Our guiding principle for the selection of pieces remains the same as it ever has been: is it interesting; and is it beautifully written? Over the years, our contributors have included the very best writers and thinkers in the world: from Virginia Woolf to Seamus Heaney, Sylvia Plath to Susan Sontag, Milan Kundera to Christopher Hitchens, Patricia Highsmith to Martin Scorsese.

The book you are holding is part of a brand-new imprint, TLS Books, by which we are striving to bring more beautiful writing to a wider public. We hope you enjoy it. If you want to read more from us, you'll find a special trial subscription offer to the *TLS* at the back of this book.

In an ever-quickening culture of flipness and facility, fake news and Facebook, the *TLS* is determined to be part of the counter-culture of quality. We believe in expertise, breadth and depth. We believe in the importance of ideas, and the transformative power of art. And we believe that, in reading the *TLS* – in whatever form, be it in a magazine, online or in a book – you are supporting a set of values that we have been proud to uphold for more than a hundred years. So thank you for that.

Stig Abell, Editor-in-Chief, TLS Books
London, 2021

Giving
a Damn

Giving a Damn

Race, Romance and Gone with the Wind

Patricia J. Williams

TLS

TLS Books
An imprint of HarperCollins*Publishers*
1 London Bridge Street
London SE1 9GF

The-TLS.co.uk

HarperCollins*Publishers*
1st Floor, Watermarque Building, Ringsend Road
Dublin 4, Ireland

First published in Great Britain in 2021 by TLS Books

1

ISBN 978-0-00-840450-5

Typeset in Publico Text
Printed and bound in Great Britain by
CPI Group (UK) Ltd, Croydon

MIX
Paper from
responsible sources
FSC™ C007454

Giving
a Damn

I. *'The Battle of Love'*

'Here was the last ever to be seen of the Knights and
their ladies Fair, of Master and of Slave [...] it is no
more than a dream remembered.'[1]

It was not a kind thought that flitted across my mind
while I waited at the airport in Montreal. The weather
was bad, my flight was late and I was having lunch on the
'American side' of the terminal, listening to a big, jovial
man talking about his son's wedding on a former cotton
plantation in Charleston, South Carolina. The man was
discussing ordinary things – the weather, the bride, the
wine served, what music they played. Everyone, he said,
was dressed in antebellum clothing: 'So much fun!' is
how he summed it up.

'*Dancing on graves!*' is what went through my mind.
And then, quick on its heels, a well-disciplined self-flagel-
lation, a socialized apologia: 'Am I being uncharitable?'

The man and his companion passed on to the vast
quantities of beer consumed at the reception. How

'rowdy, but y'know happy-rowdy' the groom's fraternity brothers grew as the night progressed and how certain he was that 'nobody slept that night, heh-heh-heh'.

The second unkind thought that passed through my mind was: 'I am so glad that neither this man nor his son nor his son's beer-guzzling frat-bros own my body.'

I suppose a bit of explanation is in order here: The overwhelming majority of African Americans are to some degree the carnal issue of precisely that 'heh-heh-heh'. I, for example, am only the third generation of my family whose body is not legally owned by others. My maternal great-grandmother was born a slave. My maternal great-grandfather was a white slaveholder who impregnated her sometime around 1860 in order to increase his livestock of plantation labourers, his stock of lives. It was not just sport to rape one's slaves: the children therefrom were valuable currency, investments in their owner's wealth by virtue of their potential for profitable divestment.

The poet Caroline Randall Williams is the great-great-granddaughter of Edmund Pettus, 'the storied Confederate general, the grand dragon of the Ku Klux Klan, the man for whom Selma's Bloody Sunday Bridge is named', as she put it in an op-ed succinctly entitled: 'You Want a Confederate Monument? My Body is a Confederate Monument' in *The New York Times* on June 26, 2020. Writing about the removal of Confederate monuments, she observed that 'there are those who dismiss the hardships of the past. They imagine a world of benevolent masters, and speak with misty eyes of gentility and honor and land. They deny plantation rape, or explain it away, or question the degree of frequency with which it occurred. To those people it is my privilege to say, *I am proof*.'

America's history is one in which Black and white families are traumatically interconnected. But that history is repressed. The pain of it echoes across generations. Nearly all Black Americans are the thoroughly mixed progeny of white slaveholders, the violence of whose paternity is variously misperceived as a biological stain, an unfortunate mutation, a legal non-fiction, a dark political taboo.

The scars of slavery's violence are hard to talk about. My mind drags the details into the present involuntarily, for, like any taboo, these feelings are deep in my autonomic system, as persistent reiteration, as terrible hallucination. 'A thing which has lost its idea is like the man who has lost his shadow, and it must either fall under the sway of madness or perish,' wrote Jean Baudrillard.[2]

Growing up, I was protected, insulated, cautioned and by some measures made paranoid by my grandmother's narrative: *They* – the always-watchful 'they'! – *might own your body, but they can never own you.* That was her sound advice, a coming to terms in the present with a very complicated past. I am safest, I learned at a very young age, when I can discipline myself to leave the body behind. It is a mystery, a kind of magic, to be raised both within and without oneself; to see and to see oneself seeing. That is the stress that W. E. B. Du Bois called 'double consciousness, this sense of always looking at one's self through the eyes of others, of measuring one's soul by the tape of a world that looks on in amused contempt and pity. One feels his two-ness, – an American, a Negro; two souls, two thoughts, two unreconciled strivings; two warring ideals in one dark body, whose dogged strength alone keeps it from being torn asunder.'[3] It is also a kind of madness – to dissociate from one's deepest organs of knowing; to cut the cord to the lifeboat of the present, and trust that past and future will form the raft upon which you might purchase your own survival.

The question continues to weigh: *Was I being uncharitable?*

The city of Charleston is known for its beautifully preserved plantations and colonial buildings. Tourism is perhaps its major industry; destination weddings and special events underwrite the maintenance costs of plantation manors. Yet Charleston's architectural charm rests on the extraordinary wealth generated by the slave trade. It is estimated that half of all slaves imported to the United States entered through Charleston's port.[4] Its history is marked by slave rebellions and the violent quashing thereof; the fear of insurrection was so great that the Security Act of 1739 specifically required all white men to carry guns to church. And like many other places in the southern United States, various laws prohibited slaves from earning money, growing their own food, practising religion, or learning to read. In 1860, South Carolina was the first state to secede from the Union; and the first battle of the Civil War took place at Fort Sumter, in Charleston's harbour.

The languorous romance of plantation life in the Deep South, of ladies in ruffled dresses and gentlemen in riding boots sipping mint juleps, is a fairy tale popularized by Margaret Mitchell's 1936 novel *Gone with the Wind*, and the 1939 film adaptation starring Clark Gable and Vivien Leigh. The tropes projected from that one work alone have had disproportionate global influence in imagining the passionate seductions of the antebellum South and the 'tragic lost cause' of the Confederacy. Despite the influence of abolitionist narratives like Harriet Beecher Stowe's *Uncle Tom's Cabin* (1852) or Frances Anne Kemble's *Journal of a Residence on a Georgian Plantation in 1838–1839* (1863), it is ultimately the apologist glossing of *Gone with the Wind* that has had the more enduring appeal. *Gone with the Wind* won the Pulitzer Prize in 1937; and a Harris poll found that, as recently as 2014, it was the second favourite book among American readers, after the Bible. It was not until the global outrage at the death of George Floyd in the spring of 2020 that Americans began to rethink the book's oversized influence in entrenching a number of racialized stereotypes: the sweep-em-off-their-feet-but-don't-give-a-damn ideal of Rhett Butler's bad-boy wooing, Scarlett O'Hara's beautiful-but-spoiled white Southern belle, and also the faithful Black Mammy-who-has-no-other-name-but-Mammy, and the figuration of slaves generally as simple, docile and happy with their lot. Among the flurry of apologetic gestures performed by American corporations after the death of George Floyd, HBO took the film version of *Gone with the Wind* off the air, because of its 'painful stereotypes' and 'racist depictions'. The film was reinstated on its streaming service a few weeks later, bracketed by an introductory 'discussion of its historical context' presented by the University of Chicago film scholar Jacqueline Stewart.

Part of *Gone with the Wind*'s popularity no doubt came from its positioning as a feel-good follow-up to the more controversial and violent defence of the Confederacy presented in Thomas Dixon's novel, *The Clansman: An Historical Romance of the Ku Klux Klan* (1905)[5] and its film adaptation, *Birth of a Nation* (1915), directed by D. W. Griffith. Wrote Dixon:

Prior to the Civil War, the Capital was ruled, by an aristocracy founded on brains, culture and blood ... Now a negro electorate controlled the city government, and gangs of drunken negroes, its sovereign citizens, paraded the streets at night firing their muskets unchallenged and unmolested ... A new mob of onion-laden breath, mixed with perspiring African odour, became the symbol of American Democracy.[6]

The Clansman culminates with celebratory descriptions of the Ku Klux Klan's victory over Yankees, scalawags, carpetbaggers and the reforms of the Freedmen's Bureau:

The secret weapon with which they struck was the most terrible and efficient in human history – these pale hosts of white-and-scarlet horsemen! They struck shrouded in a mantle of darkness and terror ... Not a single disguise was ever penetrated. All was planned and ordered as by destiny. The accused was tried by secret tribunal, sentenced without a hearing, executed in the dead of night without warning, mercy, or appeal. The movements of the Klan were like clockwork, without a word, save the whistle of the Night Hawk, the crack of his revolver, and the hoofbeat of swift

horses moving like figures in a dream, and vanish-
ing in mists and shadows.[7]

The depiction of newly-freed slaves as rapists, fools,
thieves and murderers in *Birth of a Nation* is widely cred-
ited with spurring a deadly resurgence of Klan activity
throughout the United States, resulting in increased
violence against Blacks, and the passage of Jim Crow laws
legalizing segregation. Given this social context, *Gone
with the Wind* offered the sentimental balm of plucky and
endearing Confederate heroism. And this palliative char-
acterization has only grown through the decades, and
presently underwrites much of the revisionist discourse
about race relations in America's Trumpian, supposedly
'post-race' political divide. And so we find ourselves in a
world where there are endless debates about whether
the Civil War was really about slavery at all. On some
plantation tours, slaves are referred to as 'immigrants'
and 'employees'.[8] And many of those who continue to
wave the Confederate flag claim they are merely celebrat-
ing a race-less 'Southern culture' and old-fashioned
values of good food, steadfast honour and committed
sacrifice.

But back to the 'American side' of the Canadian airport.
The father of the bridegroom and his companion seemed
like good people – happy and racially innocent, swad-
dled in a bubble of bliss, however radioactive it might

have seemed to me. I wondered again if I were being uncharitable, rueful for the thoughts I was thinking.

This kind of self-consciousness is ingrained in me by now. More than one white friend has called me 'too politically correct' to ever relax. *It is not his fault.* I am encouraged to understand that it is not a mortal sin to marry one's child off in the magnolia-scented bosom of a Confederate mansion built and serviced by invisible slaves. Why should this guilt be carried by anyone alive today: how could they know? Why *should* they know?

Recently, the *Washington Post* published a story about the discomfort some white people experience during tours of antebellum mansions in the Deep South. 'My husband and I were extremely disappointed in this tour,' wrote one online reviewer, noting that her family had never owned slaves. 'We didn't come to hear a lecture on how the white people treated slaves [...] The tour guide was so radical about slave treatment we felt we were being lectured and bashed about the slavery [...] I'll go back to Louisiana and see some real plantations that are so much more enjoyable to tour.'[9]

The matter of responsibility sent my stomach into knots. I set aside the vexed question of 'real plantations' for the moment, gently, so that I could better digest my soup.

It is true: I don't relax. This history is too resonant in my body. It irks me that we Americans continue to live in such utterly separate worlds. Scarlett O'Hara continues to float on as the brave Confederate archetype, while just beneath the surface of the plot line lurks the quiet obeisance, the persistent alterity of Big Sam and Mammy and Prissy and Pork. It's not easy for me to work up any kind of nostalgia for a style of life that depended on slaves, hierarchy, imperiousness and pomp. And I frankly despise how the tourism industry has underwritten childish rituals of antebellum dress-up in crinoline and whalebone and marketed them as romantic, swoony and gossamer.

I am no fun at all, I know.

I try to acknowledge the deep pleasure of that parent at his child's wedding and to place it in a different part of my heart from the resentment I feel about the choice of venue. I try to winnow the anger I feel about how much of that cruel history has been steamrollered into oblivion by deep-fried, honeysuckled symbolism. But the winnowing is hard work. If a majority of white Americans' knowledge of slavery comes only from *Gone with the Wind*, then they may indeed imagine a world where all but a few of the most 'loyal' slaves deployed their 'unerring African instinct' to take 'shameless advantage' of their kindly masters, telling simple-minded lies and lounging about like indolent children.[10] After all, 'there had never been a slave sold from Tara and only one whipping'.[11] In the 1996 preface to Scribner's edition of the novel, Pat

Conroy writes, 'In the structure of Margaret Mitchell's perfect society, slavery was an essential part of the unity and harmony of Southern life before Fort Sumter [...] The Ku Klux Klan plays the same romanticised role it had in *Birth of a Nation* and appears to be a benign combination of the Elks Club and a men's equestrian society.'[12] It is a world in which slaves, told that Yankees had set them free, 'indignantly' respond: 'No, Ma'am! Dey din' sot me free. Ah wouldn' let no sech trash sot me free ... Ah still b'longs ter Miss Pitty an' w'en Ah dies she gwine lay me in de Hamilton buhyin' groun' what Ah b'longs.'[13] This is an imaginary world that sets white audiences up for alarmed surprise when they learn that African Americans have always celebrated and continue to celebrate the fact of freedom. This is a continuing mindset that allows politicians like Donald Trump to state that 'nobody had ever heard of Juneteenth' (the celebration of June 19, 1865, when news of the Emancipation Proclamation arrived in Texas) until he made it 'very famous'.

Most African Americans share some intergenerationally transmitted memory of the power white owners had to hit, beat, whip, rape, or simply tear families apart by selling children, parents, loved ones 'down the river' never to be seen again. If one wants to test the dark reality of those experiences beside Mitchell's fairy tale, one can simply read Thomas Jefferson's own opinions about race, in his *Notes on the State of Virginia*, about how the

burden of such complex emotional labour falls disproportionately on Black people.[14] One can read Frances
Anne Kemble's description of her husband's lifestyle in
her *Journal of a Residence on a Georgian Plantation (1838–
1839)*.[15] One may explore the records of estate sales –
including Thomas Jefferson's – where slaves were placed
on the auction block, and sold to pay off debts.[16] Recalled
Peter Fossett, more than seventy years after the 1827
auction of Jefferson's slaves at Monticello (a lot that
included himself and all his family): '[...] after this Mr
Jefferson died. Then began our troubles. We were scattered all over the country, never to meet each other again
until we meet in another world.'[17] Similarly, after the
death of his master, Frederick Douglass wrote: 'I was
immediately sent for, to be valued with the other property.'[18]

Apart from *Narrative of the Life of Frederick Douglass,
an American Slave* (1845) or Solomon Northrup's memoir,
Twelve Years a Slave (1853), the very fact that so few Black
voices survive from slavery is, in itself, testament to the
oppressive brutality of an institution that outlawed
everything from teaching slaves to read, publishing on
their own, testifying in court, or marrying without their
master's permission. Denial of the brutality of this history
remains entrenched, with widespread assumptions that
white men must have been 'in love' with Black slave
women – and children – like Sally Hemings for there to

have been so much procreation across racial lines. There was great surprise when audiences learned that Toni Morrison's novel, *Beloved* (1987), was based on the real case of Margaret Garner, who killed her own daughter rather than surrender the child back into bondage under the Fugitive Slave Act.

Recently, the extraordinary collective reflection upon the death of George Floyd has brought a swell of interest in books about this history; as well as a surge of white people reaching out to as many Black people as they know, wondering how to help, how to learn, how to become a good ally. This is indeed a welcome development, if genuinely sustained and ultimately acted upon. I, for one, am glad to teach, remind, reveal this history for as long as it takes and to whatever degree I have something helpful to share; I look forward to joining with all curious people in unravelling together the complex and often painful tapestry of American history. I do not shy from this work, but I am cautious about how the burden of such complex emotional labour falls disproportionately on Black people.

As I write, a friend calls to apologize for something her father said in my presence thirty years ago. She apologizes for not having spoken up back then. She asks how I'm feeling about #BlackLivesMatter protests happening around the world right now. She wants to know what it's like to have a Black son. She begs my forgiveness for being so naive about the difficulties of minority existence. She wants me to know she has never thought of me in the plural, but only in the Very Special Singular. I do appreciate the kindness behind her thoughts, but I do not seek such apologies. Nor do I wish to hold myself out as someone who has the power of absolution and forgiveness of complex societal sins.

I worry that we Americans go through seasons of apology that leave us suspended and unsettled rather than focused on tough commitments to change through learning. Apologies only get us so far, and are too often haunted by associations that feel unfinished and unmoored. I am much more interested in the often uncommunicated deeper anxieties hiding behind apology, skulking behind the guilt, popping out in clumsy displays of what the author Robin DiAngelo has called 'white fragility'. Leaping from shadow, such anxiously suppressed back-door behaviour reappears ceaselessly, and ever so unintentionally. As James Baldwin wrote in his 1965 essay, 'The White Man's Guilt', 'people who imagine that history flatters them are impaled on their history like a butterfly on a pin and become incapable of seeing or changing themselves or the world'.[19] And so the 'blind-but-now-I-see' apologies fall like endless spring showers: we hope that flowers will bloom in their wake, but meanwhile ... the ground is very soggy. Consider: in 2019, Virginia Governor Ralph Northam issued a formal apology for a photo in his 1984 medical school yearbook, in either blackface or in Ku Klux Klan robes (he later recanted and said he didn't think it was a photo of him after all, but that he had donned blackface on another occasion).[20] Mere weeks later, his wife had to be pressed to apologize for handing out cotton bolls to Black children during a tour of the governor's mansion, while asking them to imagine picking the crop as slaves. 'I regret that I have upset anyone,' Ms Northam said, echoing the innocence of her husband. 'I am still committed to chronicling the important history of the Historic Kitchen, and will continue to engage historians and experts on the best way to do so in the future.'[21]

Some time ago, the artist Kevin Beasley was interviewed for a short film titled *Kevin Beasley's Raw Materials*.[22] In the film, produced by the arts non-profit Art21 and screened at the Whitney Museum in New York City, he reflected on the legacy of the cotton industry in his family's history and in the American South, asking himself, 'Why am I so mad at this plant? This plant is not doing anything except growing and being beautiful.' I completely understood the paradox. We hate the traces of slavery. No matter their innocence, the symbols summon pain. They pull a perfumed scrim over nothing less than atrocity, akin to the same reductive euphemism of those who prefer to refer to slaves as 'African immigrants' or 'indentured servants'.[23] This revisionist enchantment with plantation life has barely changed since the Civil War. In their book, *Denmark Vesey's Garden: Slavery and Memory in the Cradle of the Confederacy* (2018), Ethan Kytle and Blain Roberts observe:

> From the beginnings of postwar Charleston tourism, then African Americans were a tourist attraction, like the antiquated churches and plantations that made the area so unique. White visitors saw them – barely removed from the Old South setting at all – as a picturesque, even entertaining, aspect of the local scenery. These portraits of blacks functioned like magnolias and Spanish moss, as 'a signifier of the Old South' to northern tourists not only craving novelty but also taken with fantasies of white supremacy and black docility. In this way, the remnants of slavery, whether human or architectural, helped foster sectional reconciliation, their aesthetic attributes deflecting from their political content.[24]

This powerful nostalgia for sanitized societies that never really existed is a dominant motif in *Gone with the Wind* – and a motif that Mitchell herself plays upon. After the fall of Atlanta, while reflecting upon a future 'when she had money again', Scarlett imagines that:

There would be long warm afternoons when ladies would call and, amid the rustlings of taffeta petticoats and the rhythmic harsh cracklings of palmetto fans, when she would serve tea and delicious sandwiches and cakes and leisurely gossip the hours away. And she would be so kind to those who were suffering misfortune, take baskets to the poor and soup and jelly to the sick and 'air' those less fortunate in her fine carriage [...] Her pleasure in these thoughts of the future was undimmed by any realization that she had no real desire to be unselfish or charitable or kind. All she wanted was the reputation for possessing these qualities.[25]

The allure of the condescending languorous South doesn't only apply to historical sites. It is used to sell new sites, too. In February 2019, the sports broadcaster Warner Wolf was arrested in Naples, Florida, after defacing a sign at the entrance of the gated community where he lives, which reads 'Classics Plantation Estates'. He allegedly tore off the word 'Plantation'.[26] Without condoning the vandalism, I was nonetheless heartened. It is too rare to hear of a white person so powerfully overcome by the same historical associations that occur to so many African Americans. I felt as though 'my' history might be more generously shared as comprehensively 'ours', as pan-racially American, with plantation life seen for all its complex repercussions in (dividing) community to the present day.

This is in stark contrast to the examples of too many people who profess hearty endorsement of civil rights or anti-discrimination work, yet whose fears lurk beneath the thinnest of veneers. In July of 2020, two residents of St. Louis, Mark and Patricia McCloskey, ascended to social media infamy when they pulled guns – including an AK15 – on a group of people peacefully protesting the death of George Floyd. The protesters were merely marching past the McCloskeys' home on their way to the mayor's house located a few doors down. Yet Mark McCloskey declared 'I'm not the face of anything opposing the Black Lives Matters movement. I was a person scared for my life ... protecting my wife, my home, my hearth, my livelihood, I was the victim of a mob.'[27] The McCloskeys, who are lawyers, were exercised because the crowd had passed through a wrought iron gate at the top of the street, which according to the McCloskeys, demarcated a border between the public thoroughfare and their 'private' street. This is an impression that is not only generated by but built into the layout of some cities, perhaps nowhere more prominently than in St. Louis, where there are approximately 285 streets blocked by gates, bollards or other fanciful blockades. It is the product of what the urban planner Oscar Newman called the 'defensible space theory', a design intended to make passersby feel a sense of boundary and 'under constant observation',[28] and a central structural feature of the enduring racial segregation in that city. The sense of privacy in this street (whose residents enjoy tax-subsidized public services like police, sewer, fire and water) underwrites Mark McCloskey's fear that despite the fact that 'the protesters did not even so much as set foot on his lawn, once they set foot on Portland Place they might as well "have been in my living room"'.[29] To him, 'it was like the storming of the Bastille' by 'a large crowd of angry, aggressive people'. To him, 'I didn't care what color they were … I was frightened, I was assaulted.'[30] To him, the mere presence of the crowd was so ominous that 'I was terrified that we'd be murdered within seconds. Our house would be burned down, our pets would be killed.'[31] Mark McCloskey's fear echoed Scarlett O'Hara's, that 'The Yankees would burn it all – all!'[32]

Warner Wolf pulled down the sign on the gate of his own walled community only days after President Donald Trump delivered the 2019 State of the Union speech in which he argued for more walls, walls, walls. 'Wealthy politicians and donors push for open borders while living their lives behind walls and gates and guards,' he said, supposedly to persuade his audience of the benefits of wall-building. It is true we live in an increasingly gated society, although it is not clear that this makes us safer. We are certainly more segregated – by race, by class, by religious belief and even by age. It is unclear why more gates, more barriers, more concertina wire – to say nothing of more guns – will make a better nation rather than just a more bunkered one.

'Good fences make good neighbors,' wrote Robert Frost in his 1914 poem 'Mending Wall'. It is a line that is quoted often in current political standoffs – too often, in my opinion, because it is so commonly used flatly, absolutely, in disregard for the complexity of Frost's invocation. 'Mending Wall' is a poem about wall-mending, not entirely walling off one from another. There are breaks in Frost's wall; and his language implies respect for the other's autonomy even as neighbour joins neighbour in the effort to mend what is between them.

What was in fact between Frost and his neighbour were pastures and fields to which both were beholden. As husbands to the land, they had to negotiate what trees would take root, what creatures roam, what earth would lie fallow, what crops would be sown. Subtle as its expression may have been, Frost's poem questions the need for a wall at all, even as his neighbour insists. Their tentatively engaged separateness is in quiet but stark contrast to current political discussions: it was respectful, not hostile, as each 'makes boundaries and he breaks boundaries'.

Recently, the Chinese dissident Ai Weiwei constructed a travelling art installation entitled 'Good Fences Make

Good Neighbors', explicitly questioning the utility of walls: 'When the Berlin Wall fell, there were 11 countries with border fences and walls. By 2016, that number had increased to 70,' he observed.[33] Made up of 300 pieces scattered throughout urban environments – from a large gilded cage to a fragment of wall that can be walked through – Weiwei's message is clear: 'Any kind of wall is ridiculous, even with the Great Wall of China, it never really worked [...] It shows a kind of narrow-minded idea to divide people and create some kind of hatred between people.'[34]

And yet the construction of border walls is growing rapidly. It is as though we are retreating to some medieval notion of the nation-state as fortified castle, complete with palisades and parapets, ramparts and revetments, donjons, counterscarps, barbicans, batters and battlements. These anachronistic physical barriers are mushrooming alongside the even greater opacity of technological walls, rapidly enclosing our minds and bodies by walling us biometrically, by geolocation, by electronic surveillance, by data mining. Still, it is startling how much investment has been put into very old-fashioned forms of confinement – steel, razor wire, concrete, stone – whether in Hungary, Botswana, Korea, Israel, India, China, Austria or Slovenia. From some perspectives it would seem an ineffective, expensive and ecologically disastrous solution to political problems, against which walls cannot defend. (In southeastern Arizona, President Trump is building a thirty-foot-high section of border wall straight through the San Bernardino National Wildlife Refuge. 'Once completed, for the first time in US history, the barrier will physically wall off the majority of New Mexico, Arizona and California, an area stretching from the Rio Grande to the Pacific Ocean [...] a tragedy for the border communities that call the region home as well as the more than 93 endangered and threatened species that live in this desert.'[35] The National Butterfly Center also faces a dubious future; the planned wall would run straight through it, creating a 150-foot 'enforcement zone' requiring the clearing of trees and brush and any other vegetation near it. 'The enforcement zone will be lit up all night long, threatening nocturnal wildlife and the center's economic future.'[36] There is something about this image that calls to mind the walls of the concentration camp at Majdanek: In 1946, Elisabeth Kübler-Ross visited and saw hundreds of images of butterflies etched into the walls, scratched into the stone by children who knew they were about to die.[37]

This vision of America as physically partitioned brings to mind the data artist Josh Begley's 'Prison Map', an installation of aerial photos of federal prisons.[38] 'What does the geography of incarceration look like in the United States?' Begley asks. What indeed. When I first saw his displays of satellite images, I was struck by their measured symmetry, by the geometric beauty of circles and heart-shapes and octagons etched into green land-scapes, envisioned from space. To me, the 'geography of incarceration' looks very much like the blueprints for Versailles, or floor plans for Buckingham Palace, imperi-ally grand in aspiration, ironically elegant in the filigreed detail of their ambition. Then too, they looked a lot like aerial images of President Trump's 'Florida White House' and golf club, Mar-a-Lago. When seen from outer space, the details disappear. But of course the devil is always in the details.

Images taken by astronauts from space and published by NASA show that the walls between nations can fool the eye; they resemble fiery rivers, or giant snakes, or the veins in a beautifully glimmering membrane. The wall between India and Pakistan, for example is floodlit for hundreds of miles, lending it a volcanically orange lustre, like seeping, glowing lava. These seemingly organic threading, spreading lines of demarcation are a wonder to behold at night, if only from afar.

There are so many double-edged ironies in 'protecting the neighbourhood' via this newly ramped-up project of division by wall. Walls regulate not only which bodies may cross a border, they regulate who can see beyond and who can see within. Those who build and maintain the barriers retain the capacity to survey broad land-scapes without being identified, keeping 'the other' in sight as well as at bay.[39] In 2019, President Trump claimed the business of wall-building as an 'emergency power', subject to little oversight or regulation. Technologically enhanced surveillance – whether in the form of an electronic cattle-fence with the power notched up to snare humans, or the direct glare of a CCTV camera – is an intense form of scrutiny that begs to be moderated by mutual engagement and by procedural accountability. Historically, the absence thereof has led to terrible miscarriages of justice, as Nicholas Mirzeoff reminds us: 'Under segregation, a person (of color) could be accused of "reckless eyeballing" meaning an improper look at a white person, presumed to have sexual intent [...] In the prison-industrial complex, "don't eyeball me" is still a routine instruction. The state marks its secrets "eyes only".' Fairness has always demanded the ability to confront and cross-examine the witnesses against us – nothing more, in other words than the right to know and to see who is seeing us.[40]

Both Josh Begley and Nicholas Mirzeoff advocate for 'the right to look back', as in the right to return the gaze. In an age of satellite surveillance, this also means 'the right to look up', to look aloft at the night sky and see, if we might, how much the North Star is obscured by the distant blinking and data-gathering twinkling of military aircraft and corporately funded space stations. Neither

Harriet Tubman nor the von Trapps would have made it very far in today's world.

From a distance, from a certain aesthetic remove, the antebellum plantations of the Old South are undeniably beautiful – flowering, gracefully constructed, with seemingly benevolent stretches of fields and lawns, perfect for weddings. But looking closer, we remember they're built on human degradation, even as they live on as icons of romance premised on the fragile privilege of racial innocence and historical oblivion.

II. 'The Supreme Test'

'The South was too beautiful a place to be let go
without a struggle, too loved to be trampled by
Yankees who hated Southerners enough to enjoy
grinding them into the dirt, too dear a homeland
to be turned over to ignorant people drunk with
whisky and freedom.'[1]

The tradition of Great Books has long been vexed by
questions of politics. Does a masterful writerly form
trump despicable content? Does persuasive romance
mask outright propaganda? Is fiction wholly a retreat
from material life or is it mental practice for real-world
encounters? If books regarded as classics refer to worlds
of normative nativism, racism, misogyny, religious bias
or other prejudice, what is our responsibility as readers,
as consumers, as parents, or as educators who pass such
works on to the next generation as instructive, as worthy
of study? When do we embrace or erase, expand, amend
or rewrite?

Some have attempted to separate literature from politics altogether, relegating literature to the category of 'entertainment' or skill with pretty words or the ability to craft alternative universes that provide escape from the material world rather than commentary upon it. But of course all literature is the product of its time and culture. The degree to which fictional worlds recapitulate non-fictional circumstance as well as create new worlds is simply the function of language and the semiotics of culture. In his introduction, Pat Conroy claims that he was shaped as a novelist because of his mother's fixation with Scarlett O'Hara:

> [M]y mother treated the book as though it were a manual of etiquette whose *dramatis personae* she presented as blood relations and kissing cousins rather than as creations of one artist's imagination [...] My mother could align our small universe precisely with *Gone with the Wind* and she could do it effortlessly while stirring the creamed corn. Once she had read the novel, it lived inside her the rest of her life, like a bright lamp she could always trust in the darkness.[2]

The power of imagined worlds to summon associations that are not truly fiction is a paradox that is inevitably political. In broad terms, 'imagination is more than mere fantasy: it is the capacity to produce images [...] independently of the fact of whether what they represent actually exists or not'.[3]

Pat Conroy concludes that *'Gone with the Wind* works because it possesses the inexpressible magic where the art of pure storytelling rises above its ancient use and succeeds in explaining to a whole nation how it came to be.'[4] These days we refer to that slushily disobedient resonance beyond the limits of genre as 'the culture wars'. And it is nothing new. The reason Princeton University removed President Woodrow Wilson's name from its School of Public and International Affairs in the summer of 2020 was because of Wilson's hearty endorsement of the Ku Klux Klan and Jim Crow laws, a stance in part traceable to the literary suasions of his lifelong friend, the novelist and playwright Thomas Dixon. In *The Clansman*, Dixon wrote of two 'gigantic negroes' with 'kinky heads, black skin, thick lips, white teeth and flat noses', 'crouched down on their haunches' on either side of the abolitionist 'Old Commoner' (a fictionalized figure patterned after the Radical Republican Congressman Thaddeus Stevens, whom Dixon denounces by name in the book's introduction for his 'bold attempt' to 'Africanize' the Southern states[5]):

> No sculptor ever dreamed a more sinister emblem of the corruption of a race of empire builders than this group. Its black figures, wrapped in the night of four thousand years of barbarism, squatted there the 'equal' of their master, grinning at his forms of justice, the evolution of forty centuries of Aryan genius.[6]

'History written with lightning,' was President Wilson's notorious appraisal of *The Clansman*.[7] Wilson even wrote several title cards for *Birth of a Nation*: 'The white men were roused by a mere instinct of self-preservation,' reads one. The relative vehemence of the culture wars – the battles either to monumentalize or to deconstruct any received canon – is ever a thermometer of our times.

In the United States, this staple of academic debate has grown into bitter standoffs ranging from stifling anti-intellectualism to book-banning to book-burning. As recently as 2019, white students at Georgia Southern University burned the novel *Make Your Home Among Strangers*, by the Cuban-American author Jennine Capó Crucet. The theme of the book was the difficulty of a first-generation Latina struggling to fit in at a mostly white college. Crucet had spoken on the campus earlier that day, asserting that white and non-white students have very different experiences in such educational settings. She had called for more conversation to bridge divisions. As she described it, the talk was 'an act of love and an attempt at deeper understanding'.[8] Instead, Crucet was accused by some students of reverse racism by suggesting that whiteness is privileged at all in American society. In addition to the book-burning, she received so many hateful trolls that a follow-up event the next day was cancelled because 'the administration said they could not guarantee my safety or the safety of its students on campus because of open-carry laws'.[9]

It is quite the imperfect storm these days. Some states' laws permit gun-owners to carry their weapons into classrooms, shopping malls, hospitals, gyms, bars and onto buses. All this in a climate of increasing political vitriol, where groups condemn not merely the substance of what is written, but also advocate for the physical destruction of the books and websites in which those words appear. As emotions grew heated before the 2020 Iowa Caucus leading up to the presidential election, Iowa State University banned students from 'political chalk talk' – or the habit of chalking political messages and slogans on campus. The sidewalks had become a pitched battleground; there were so many racist, antisemitic, anti-immigrant, neo-Nazi slogans blooming on walkways that the university felt that the divisiveness being generated was too great to continue to permit. Needless to say, the new battle became whether that administrative action was an encroachment on free speech.

PATRICIA J. WILLIAMS

Recently, I discovered that an essay of mine is in an anthology that has been banned from public schools in Tucson, Arizona. The anti–ethnic studies law passed in 2010 by the state (Arizona Revised Statutes Section 15–112) prohibits teachings that 'promote the overthrow of the United States government', 'promote resentment toward a race or class of people', 'are designed primarily for pupils of a particular ethnic group', and/or 'advocate ethnic solidarity instead of the treatment of pupils as individuals'. I invite you, o gentle reader, to read the book in question, titled *Critical Race Theory: An Introduction*, by Richard Delgado and Jean Stefancic, so that you may decide for yourselves whether it qualifies. In fact, I invite you to take on as your own summer reading the astonishingly lengthy list of books that have been removed from the Tucson public school system as part of this wholesale and intentional elimination of the Mexican-American studies curriculum. The banned authors and editors include Isabel Allende, Junot Díaz, Jonathan Kozol, Rudolfo Anaya, bell hooks, Sandra Cisneros, James Baldwin, Howard Zinn, Rodolfo Acuña, Ronald Takaki, Jerome Skolnick and Gloria Anzaldúa. Even Thoreau's 'Civil Disobedience' and Shakespeare's *The Tempest* received the hatchet, deemed works that are 'biased, political and emotionally charged', or where 'race, ethnicity and oppression are central themes'.

Trying to explain what was so offensive as to warrant killing the entire curriculum and firing its director, a Tucson School Board member named Michael Hicks stated rather proudly that he was not actually familiar with the curriculum. 'I chose not to go to any of their classes,' he told Al Madrigal on *The Daily Show*. 'Why even go? Why even go? I base my thoughts on hearsay from others ...'[10] Asked about the relative dangers posed by Mexican-American studies as compared to a curriculum that purports to teach the history of slavery, Mr Hicks opined that 'Rosa Clark [he apparently meant Rosa Parks] did not take out a gun and go onto a bus and hold up everybody ...'[11] Judging from Mr Hicks' remarks, it seems that Tucson had failed in its teaching of the history of slavery and the civil rights movement too.

Happily, there was significant pushback against this particular instance of anti-intellectualism. One of the most vibrant examples is a protest group called Librotraficante, or Book Trafficker, organized by Tony Diaz, a Houston Community College professor. The group has been caravanning throughout the Southwest holding readings, setting up book clubs, establishing 'underground libraries' and dispensing donated copies of the books that had been removed from Arizona's public school curriculum. A lawsuit was waged, and in 2017, a federal court struck down the book ban and permitted the restoration of the Mexican studies programme.[12]

The struggle in Arizona is not an isolated phenomenon. In addition to book-banning, things are made worse by a nationwide disparagement of teachers, teachers' unions and scholarship itself. Brooke Harris, a beloved 'teacher of the year' at Michigan's Pontiac Academy for Excellence, was summarily fired after asking – merely asking – for permission to let her students conduct a fundraiser for the family of Trayvon Martin, an African American boy who was killed by a member of a community watch for being 'suspicious'.[13]

There are a number of factors at play in these controversies. One is the frequent misuse of the right to free speech as a shield over which to lob intentionally fiery word-bombs of intolerance and hate. But another is a power to suppress speech which is too often exercised with a maddeningly confident sense of superiority that allows someone to pass sweeping judgement on a body of work without having done any study at all. After the *Chronicle of Higher Education* published an item highlighting the dissertations of five young PhD candidates in African American studies at Northwestern University, a blogger for the *Chronicle*, Naomi Schaefer Riley, wrote that the mere titles of the dissertations – about topics ranging from race in housing policy to infant mortality – were sufficient cause to eliminate all Black studies classes as 'left wing victimization claptrap'.[14] Riley hadn't read the dissertations; they hadn't even been published yet. When questioned about this, she argued that, as 'a journalist [...] it is not my job to read entire dissertations before I write a 500-word piece about them', adding, '[T]here are not enough hours in the day or money in the world to get me to read a dissertation on historical black midwifery.' Riley tried to justify her view with a clichéd plaint about the humanities and higher education: 'Such is the state of academic research these days. [...] The publication topics become more and more irrelevant and partisan. No one reads them.'[15] This is not mere arrogance; it is the same cocooned, 'white-ghetto' narrow-mindedness that allows Michael Hicks to be in charge of a major American school system yet not know 'Rosa Clark's' real name.

III. 'Across the Chasm'

'While they were unconscious, the world had
changed. The Yankees had come, the darkies had
gone and Mother had died. Here were three
unbelievable happenings and their minds could not
take them in.'[1]

From time to time, I have a dream in which I am fleeing northward. It's perhaps not a surprising dream – to African Americans, 'north' remains a cipher for freedom. The Underground Railroad deployed all sorts of secret codes and opaque signs to mark the paths from slave states to free states, or ultimately to Canada. Even after slavery, Blacks like my grandparents escaping lynching and repression by fleeing Jim Crow states, headed mostly north; my grandmother and her sisters were part of that migration, from Tennessee to Massachusetts, in the late 1800s. There are still traces of that flight retained in popular culture references: the polestar points the way to better opportunities. Look to the heavens, the Big Dipper will guide you. Follow the drinking gourd.

I think about the quiet loneliness of such images, the stealth required to leave the confines of home, to cross borders, to get one's body elsewhere – before a petulant master moved your body for you, like a mute, wooden chess piece. Frederick Douglass wrote of one slave whose concern about being overworked reached his master's ears: '[F]or having found fault with his master, he was now to be sold to a Georgia trader. He was immediately chained and handcuffed; and thus, without a moment's warning, he was snatched away, and forever sundered, from his family and friends, by a hand more unrelenting than death. This is the penalty of telling the truth, of telling the simple truth [...] It is partly in consequence of such facts that slaves, when inquired of as to their condition and the character of their masters, almost universally say they are contented, and that their masters are kind.'[2] But behind those obedient faces, people read the stars – pointing to Canada or as close to it as possible. Canada was the end of the rainbow, the cynosure.

This was an imaginary Canada, of course. The travel from slavery to freedom was only partly about geography; and the trauma of fleeing home to find home has been passed down through generations and still disturbs my sleep, no matter where I am on the planet. I am surely not alone in the dream of constant flight. The United

States is not only the happy stew of migrant histories we so euphemistically call a 'melting pot'; it is also a site of mourning, a home for the homeless, a repository for colonialism's lost souls. We tend to think of the American Dream as a magnet of economic prosperity; but the full story of American identity is a tapestry of tales of displacement, escape, belonging, resentment, conflict and survival. These narratives are often violently incompatible yet they are laid over each other, co-existing within the same bodies. Emma Lazarus's poetic inspiration is engraved on the Statue of Liberty: 'Give me your tired, your poor, your huddled masses yearning to breathe free, the wretched refuse of your teeming shore. Send these, the homeless, tempest-tossed to me, I lift my lamp beside the golden door!' ('The New Colossus', 1883). But those lines are dogged by parallel ideologies like those embedded in Iowa Representative Steve King's recent call to white nationalism: 'We can't restore our civilization with somebody else's babies.' When President Donald Trump began his first term with an inauguration speech that summoned spectres of 'American carnage', he awakened a terrible restlessness in the American polity: a furiously competitive survivalism that has turned the wanderer's search for safe haven into a turf war. In August 2019, Ken Cuccinelli, then the acting head of US Citizenship and Immigration Services, told NPR that the poem ought to read: 'Give me your tired, your poor who can stand on their own two feet and who will not become a public charge.' And to clarify any lingering confusion, Cuccinelli added, 'Of course, that poem was referring back to people coming from Europe ...'

Mobility and escape have been central in American mythology, but its promise expands and contracts with time and region. Some of us tell stories of moving northward, others describe romantic caravans to the Wild West, many are in love with the notion of motion itself and take to our cars and the open road with no particular destination in mind. She has come to memorialize a frozen past, but Scarlett O'Hara's one great strength was her ability to move forward through time, to leave the past behind and head future-ward, for 'tomorrow is another day'. If my family moved according to compass points, other Americans speak of mobility as an economic direction, a ladder, a spire, a path of gold that leads upward – always and inevitably upward as though towards heaven. We Americans are wanderers and transplants. We travel light, toward that North Star – even our families are 'nuclear'. We 'flip' houses; we 'reinvent' ourselves; we skip grades; we climb mountains; we lift ourselves up; we pass through.

This mythology was only sustainable, however, so long as it was underwritten by romantic fictions of endless space and empty vistas waiting to be conquered, a world where boundless ambition has no cost and the future no horizon. But the world is not infinite; and rootlessness implies a troubling lack of connection to the place or to the ecosystems through which we move. The blowback from such adventurism has resulted in another feature of American history: fear of precisely such freedom of movement, whether of slave rebellion or immigrant invasion or foreign contagion. This fear has rendered us Americans blind to the degree to which we are a nation densely honeycombed with fences, barriers, segregated neighbourhoods, mass incarceration, gated communities, walls and The Wall.

Whether because of income inequality or climate change or the defunding of education or lack of basic health care, Americans are facing a crisis of identity, born of rigid segregation in nearly every sphere of society. It is not my aim here to address only race or class or migration or homelessness, but rather to think about some of the conceptions that have brought what is arguably the richest and most diverse nation on the planet to the brink of such resurgent, violent division. How did we – who so love moving – end up so 'balkanized'? How did we squander the political will that surged during the civil rights movement to find ourselves facing today's state of urgent and disgraceful domestic deterioration? What has happened, in the fluctuating tension of American narratives, to allow Steve King's vision its current political ascendancy over Emma Lazarus's?

The sense of encroaching danger that requires we put walls between people seems to have inspired a certain *schadenfreude* about the necessity for extralegal, even anti-legal, resolution. The wildly disproportionate circulation of pictures of a ravaged America endlessly at risk from Mexican rapists, African American thuggery and Muslim terrorists has corrupted our discourse. Increasingly we speak to each other through a densely imagined fog where harsh punishments must be dealt out, and gleeful retribution wreaked upon dark bodies. Moreover, we have collectively given new life to a reconstructed narrative of warrior masculinity that ultimately dates back to *Birth of a Nation* – the trope of a strong, pugilistic white vigilante fighting against corrupt, lying and libertine Black invaders (literally Black voters in that movie) – in order to protect the honour of frightened white women from terrorists and 'very bad people' who have escaped from 'certain neighborhoods'.[3]

The crises of the last few years have also inspired much resistance to vigilantism and excessive use of force by law enforcement; that resistance has coalesced into conversations and activism such as #BlackLivesMatter and the #MeToo movement. But among a broad spectrum of Americans, attempts to draw attention to overlooked voices and unnecessary deaths among a disproportion of Black people seem to degrade quickly into contests between whether 'our lives' matter as much as 'their

lives' – or worse, whether 'my people' have any obliga-
tion to extend the perquisites of either citizenship or due
process to those marked undesirable, or parasitic or
Lebensunwertes Leben.[4]

As we come now to the likely edge of a period of
extended emergency and normalized suspensions of law,
it is worth tracking the emotional and gestural language
that enables this undoing, and what might lie beyond.
There are powers gathering force that have been mixing
a newly toxic brew of anti-law, culture wars and outright
violence. We see vicious new norms of incivility, based
on old resentments, but enhanced by new technologies
that spread anger with the efficiency of wildfire –
technologies that nullify fact, nullify inconvenient
statistics, nullify presumptions of innocence, nullify jury
instructions and make due process seem a luxury we
cannot afford. High-powered immigrant bashing and
mean-spirited populism seem to have swept across many
parts of the US – fuelled by trolls, bots and social media,
effectively reconstituting animosities that date back to
centuries of colonial expansion. Increasingly we see
predictive models of policing based on 'likely' behaviour,
group profiling and segregation based on suspicion
rather than conviction, and a predisposition to literally
shoot first, ask questions later. Patrick J. Lynch, president
of the New York City Police Department's police union,
has repeatedly endorsed this notion of so-called

'proactive policing'; indeed, police officials across the country openly embrace this blatantly unconstitutional concept of presumed guilt. And after camouflaged federal troops snatched citizens off the streets of Portland, Oregon and held them without charge in July, 2020, Chad Wolf, acting head of the Department of Homeland Security defended this deploy because 'we are having to go out and proactively arrest individuals. And we need to do that because we need to hold them accountable.'[5] This mode of political address is often couched in talk of 'law and order' but it privileges order above all. It endows shape, form, flesh to an ever-loudening thrum of calls for 'a new civil war'.[6]

On January 20, 2020, tens of thousands of gun owners – many bearing large military-style semi-automatic weapons, sniper rifles and side arms – converged on the state capitol building in Richmond, Virginia. They were protesting proposed gun-control legislation, and the rally became a show of civilian force unlike any other in American history. The organizers assured the media that this was to be a celebration of the Second Amendment, at which all were welcome. But it was embraced by enough far-right extremist groups – QAnon, the Base, the Oathkeepers, neo-Nazis – that the Governor of Virginia, Ralph Northam, declared a state of emergency. The event was peaceful however; police and demonstrators were filmed chatting calmly and smiling together. Attendees seemed festive, waving Trump posters and flags that said 'Build the Wall'. While it seems to me hard to call that much weaponry a show of anything like peace, the day went off without a hitch, despite some arrests beforehand of people who had allegedly planned to bring a few bombs and use the occasion to start that civil war.

At the same time, this rally was significant for a great deal more than lobbying the legislature. Despite a few T-shirts that advocated Black gun ownership, the attendees were nearly all white. The event took place on a federal holiday officially honouring Dr Martin Luther King, Jr. It took place in Richmond, the former capital of the Confederate States of America. The not irrational fear of violent confrontation kept many people away, particularly people of colour. Businesses had to close because employees were afraid to come to work. Yet the President tweeted his support of the event, writing 'The Democrat Party in the Great Commonwealth of Virginia are working hard to take away your 2nd Amendment rights. This is just the beginning. Don't let it happen, VOTE REPUBLICAN in 2020.'[7]

That spectacle of brandished heavy weaponry against the backdrop of the old Confederacy still weighed on many minds a few weeks later, when the President tweeted his opinion of the Academy of Motion Picture Arts and Sciences' award of the Oscar for Best Picture to the film *Parasite*: 'And the winner is a movie from South

Korea. What the hell was that all about? We've got enough problems with South Korea, with trade. And after all that they give them best movie of the year? Was it good? I don't know. Y'know I'm like looking for, let's get *Gone with the Wind*, can we get like *Gone with the Wind* back, please?'[8]

It is hard to know what to make of all this. With Donald Trump's presidency, disregard for rigorously vetted data, for the judiciary, for due process, diplomatic convention and human rights has metastasized into a full-blown constitutional emergency. What for a time seemed xenophobia specifically aimed at impoverished migrants from Latin and Central America morphed into a war against 'aliens' writ large. What for a time seemed a specific if disproportional fear of illegal border crossings has morphed into a war against the very legitimacy of asylum-seeking itself. And while the sense of alarm is focused on the southern border with Mexico, the reality is that more drugs and other contraband are smuggled in from Canada than from Mexico. In other words, President Trump's inflammatory images of gangs and drug mules pouring into Texas and Arizona comport more with the statistical realities of what is happening along the northern border.

I cannot help but see the bodies of my near ancestors in the current caravans of desperate souls fleeing from place to place, chased by famine, war and toxins. 'The bodies of my ancestors' may sound romantic or trite, but I take that idea seriously. I am not speaking here of biologized inheritance: my epigenetics, my predispositions for depression or resilience. Instead, I mean the inheritance of language – the linguistically and rhetorically embedded traditions passed on in habits of speech. I am composed of the voices of those who bred me. We are talked into the world by our forebears: by how they parsed words or not at all, how they charmed, seduced, talked back or over, how or if they were heard at all. Their emotional inflections, their instincts for fight or flight inhabit us, inhabit me. Their accented soundscape is the familiarity through which we filter all experience. It is an idea of home, even when groundless, or unsupported by structure, or bereft of actual landscape. I became a lawyer because I am still running towards the whispered promise of justice.

When anyone's sense of home is endangered or unsettled by a persistent history of trauma, there can be a certain fixedness about one's origin story, a determination to reproduce only the noblest dreams of one's forefathers. While recording an episode of the television show *American Roots* for example, the actor Ben Affleck was confronted with historical evidence that his ancestors were slave owners. Aghast, he somehow convinced the Public Broadcasting Corporation not to air that particular bit of information.[9] In a culture where there are no neighbourhood griots to keep us honest over generations and only a premium on radical individualism, we place great pride on will-power as our only truth. Anthropologist Alondra Nelson has aptly named this instinct for denialism 'genealogical disorientation'.[10] Similarly, in pursuit of political perfection, we may suffer what might be called data disorientation. President Trump continues to deny climate change even as Mar-a-Lago, his winter estate in Florida, sinks into the sea. We tend to live in the conditional as though it were the present: culturally, we are encouraged to imagine ourselves as CEOs or basketball stars or living on Mars with little more preparation than a wish and a banner that reads 'Mission Accomplished'. We Americans 'stand our ground' even when there is little in the way of ground to stand upon.

But our legacy is one of human exploitation and resource depletion. Frederick Douglass – and many of our great-grandparents – passed down memories of masters and mistresses who murdered their slaves for falling asleep or learning to read or whipped them simply for pique or for sport. It is a violent past of both boundary-transgression and boundary-imposition: of action for action's sake with little value placed on reflection, pause, hesitation or question. The collective fear of a transgressive other (which extends to a fear of transgressive 'each-others' or intimates) has made us both trigger-happy and nostalgic for the imagined peace of our idealized Edenic origins. This longing for a fabricated past of pure perfection has crystallized into thousands of fundamentalist formations which keep us separated from one another: clubs, sects, parties, cults, armies, tribes, splinters, orthodoxies, gangs, chat rooms, blood vengeance, blood bonds, to say nothing of Fox News. To acknowledge slavery is to acknowledge our collective vulnerability and this leaves us all scrambling for an exoskeleton to call home.

It may be helpful to understand American attitudes towards identity and place as linked to a deep ambivalence about the notion of home, not simply a lack of physical shelter. It may be useful to consider whether most of us Americans have ever really been able to enjoy a developed sense of place. Perhaps we are not nomads by choice. Perhaps we move because we feel chased. As President Trump exemplifies with every tweet, perhaps we carry a perpetual sense of siege within us. We have little sustained practice in the art of neighbourliness, and that lack has an undertow ripe for exploitation at this moment in time: We are no longer largely an agrarian economy of family-owned enterprise; our economic existence is urban, suburban, and dominantly linked to a service economy that can push too many of us out into the cold at will, with little notice and few benefits. When we have trouble with another human being we fire them, we quit, we shut the door, we pack up and leave the neighbourhood, we build a higher wall. It is no longer possible to reduce this to an inherited sense of restlessness, in other words: we are indeed being chased from our abodes. Our ability to find places to rest and raise a family are under siege in new and unfamiliar ways that impact not merely people of colour but mainstream middle-class white Americans, too, who expected the promise of 'infinity and beyond!'[11] to bless them as beneficently as during the gold rush or the gilded age or when cotton was king.

In finally coming face-to-face with the limit on places to run, we also come face-to-face with each other as though for the first time. The sudden encroachment of the unpleasant reality that we are all in the same boat – that is, the same neighbourhood, the same nation, the same planet – is jarring, and frightening. Perhaps it is not surprising that that sense of vulnerability and exposure would feed racist, fundamentalist and nativist impulses to wall in the neighbourhood, wall off the nation and wall out that intruding other world. There is no North Star to follow to a promised land. In a world ablaze with the bright lights of surveillance apparatus, there is not even a visible night sky.

Of course the entire globe has grown increasingly diasporic – out of desperate circumstance not merely a yearning for upward mobility. We are collectively rocked by the repercussions of colonial violence. Those children

Steve King so cruelly describes as 'somebody else's' *are* our progeny. They *are* our babies, and not just in humanist or universalist terms. The Central American children being detained and separated from their parents at the Mexican border represent the legacy of American policies that are decades old. After all, it was the United States that financed the infamous US Army School of the Americas and trained genocidal warlords, such as Efraín Ríos Montt, who went on to destabilize almost all of Central America. If countries like Guatemala and Honduras have fallen into chaos since the 1980s, it's partly because those wars took a toll on their social structures: the trauma of families wiped out and entire villages destroyed. The refugees at our southern border are just some of the people still seeking safety from US-financed violence.

IV. 'The Snare of the Fowler'

'Why be an ostrich?'[1]

We live in a world where there is an unprecedented planetary circulation of vulnerable bodies; and quite deadly, contagious belief systems. When there is no safe space to call home, no shelter in which to settle one's body, there can be no real commitment to a group of people, place or power.

With my magical American passport, I have not had experiences that would allow me to fully apprehend the Somalian refugee Warsan Shire's conviction that

> no one leaves home unless home chases you
> fire under feet
> hot blood in your belly
> it's not something you ever thought of doing
> until the blade burnt threats into
> your neck
> and even then you carried the anthem under

your breath
only tearing up your passport in an airport toilet
sobbing as each mouthful of paper
made it clear that you wouldn't be going back.

you have to understand,
that no one puts their children in a boat
unless the water is safer than the land[2]

I live on a patch of ground my grandmother deemed safe, a place she thought free and quiet enough to sustain a line of progeny. I have been the lucky recipient of that bet she took. The land is unsafe on much of the planet and it is a hard thing when one's familiar place, one's perceived birthright, is also a mortally dangerous space. You flee. But when groundless and stateless, one's body becomes one's only identity.

At the end of 2018, according to the UN, there were approximately seventy million refugees, asylum seekers, stateless or other persons of concern in the world – more than at any other time in history. According to the United Nations, more than 18,000 migrants have drowned attempting to cross the Mediterranean since 2014. It is unknown how many deaths occur in the desert along the US Mexico border because the Department of Homeland Security does not keep count; and it does not attempt to identify the bodies it finds in the desert. Astonishingly, we do not even seem to keep track of how many migrants have died while *in the custody* of Border Patrol: when questioned by Congress in 2018 after the death of a 7-year-old Mayan girl, Kirstjen Nielsen, then secretary of Homeland Security, simply did not know the figures.

And so a vicious circle: parents attempt to flee violence with their children; that flight is deemed illegal; that illegality marks parents as criminals not worthy of raising children; their children are removed, sometimes as 'deterrence' to others seeking asylum in the US, sometimes because the mere attempt to seek inclusion is predetermined as moral failure, inadequacy, invasion. Moreover, the construction of detention camps has been outsourced to profiteers who have snatched babies away so carelessly that their identities have been lost in the shuffle, and that 'many may never be rejoined'.[3] Of those children lost in the system, an undetermined but significant number seem to have ended up in the foster care and adoption network of Bethany Christian Services, a conservative Protestant religious agency financially linked to the US Education Secretary Betsy DeVos and her family foundation.

In June of 2020, US District Court Judge Dolly Gee ordered the release of children held with their families in immigration jails which 'are on fire' with Covid-19. '[T]here is no more time for half measures,' she wrote.[4] Half measures indeed. The response from the Trump administration's lawyers for Immigration and Customs Enforcement (ICE) was like some evil version of King Solomon's offer to slice the baby in half: ICE seemingly acceded to the release of children, but not their parents: 'The remedy for a constitutional violation of conditions of confinement is to remedy the violation, not to release petitioners.'[5] In effect, ICE's proposed remedy would present detained families with the false 'choice' of either releasing only the children, thus traumatizing them by separating them from their parents, or of keeping them all together in dense, unsafe, underfunded detention centres ridden with a deadly contagion for which there is no cure.

It is hard not to hear in this the echo of Frederick Douglass's sorrow that, born a slave, he knew neither his age nor his birthday nor his mother – for it was routine that 'before the child has reached its twelfth month, its mother is taken from it, and hired out on some farm a considerable distance off, and the child is placed under the care of an old woman, too old for field labor'.[6]

What are the origins of the immigration travesty in the US? One could start with the Crusades. Or the troubles in Ireland. Or the Ottomans. Or fascination with romantic crops like cotton, tea, rubber, coffee. Or the Cherokee Trail of Tears. Or slavery. Or the Ku Klux Klan. Or Stalin. Or Jim Crow or Japanese internment or Suharto's genocide or the refusal to shelter asylum seekers aboard the ship *St. Louis* who were fleeing Hitler during World War

II. None of this began, in other words with President Trump's so-called Muslim ban and one fears it won't end with the detention of children in military detention camps. I struggle with how to think our way out of this moment. When did it become acceptable to institutional-ize children or to massively incarcerate millions – millions! – of men and women as the US does – a country with the largest prison population in the world, and the highest per-capita incarceration rate? How did this become a naturalized, normative assortment of populations, done in the name of public interest? How did this become our resting point?

Perhaps we ought to look more closely at the details of how we live, what we do without noticing, without think-ing, the innocence of the walls between us, the sleepwalking within and without our educational systems, the dreamy slurry we move in that makes the cruelties of incarceration, both large and small, seem not quite real. So many of our most creative designs remain stagnant, so much of our kindest envisioning seems stuck in sleep, in dream, in hope, rather than in emancipatory labour. Seismic events are happening all around us. I don't know how to address everything, but here is where I start – small, with just me, doing the thinking I can do. Perhaps all any of us can hope for is to offer a helpful prism, a spark and motivation that will join with other thoughts and become vibrant.

So here's one very small thing with which I will begin. Recently I was at the gym watching TV. It was some home improvement show or another – one of those programmes where the hosts help people fix up their houses, often to sell them or buy new ones that better fit their needs. There are a lot of these shows and they're quite entertaining. Yet fun as they are, in all of them, one sees the uncomfortable realities of the American landscape: that is, the neighbourhoods are always quite segregated. This is particularly apparent in the segments where they invite supposedly random buyers in to look at a recently renovated house. If the current owner is Black, the future or potential purchaser will almost always be all Black. If the current resident is white, the potential purchasers, the visitors to the open house, will almost always be all white.

Residential segregation is, of course, not the product of personal choice. It is not because African Americans or Puerto Ricans or Jews or Koreans or Chinese or South Asians or Italians always and forever just want to live together. Sometimes, and maybe. But more often it is the product of a frequently forgotten and strenuously denied history of prejudice: of not welcoming certain others as neighbours. With regard to African Americans it is also the product of an aggressive history of 'red-lining' via federal and state policies regarding banking and the distribution of mortgages and the racially biased assignment of the benefits of the GI Bill.[7] It is also the end result of quasi-private practices like 'steering' by realtors and racially restrictive covenants.[8] If these practices are officially illegal, they have nonetheless left their enduring mark on all of us.

An Ethiopian friend of mine lives in a very high-end apartment building in New York City that was having an open house. She decided to attend because she wanted to get design ideas for her own apartment, wanted to look at the window treatments. She introduced herself to some of the potential buyers as a resident. The realtor was deeply distressed by this. The realtor felt that the presence of my friend lowered the property values, and chided the management company for not having informed them before that there were Blacks living in the building. The realtor felt 'blindsided'. How can they expect to get top dollar?

My friend, who learned about this indirectly and after the fact, was also blindsided. She felt it as her inauguration into the reality of prejudice in the US. She sought out her African American friends afterward – *Is this a thing?* she asked. She had felt quite culturally distinct and apart from the American Black experience until then. Even superior. But this hurt her feelings in a way that made her distrust her own emotions. *Everyone was so nice*, she said. The fact that she had been exceptionalized when she had moved in – perhaps because of her pretty British accent – had left her unprepared for the fact that she might ever be viewed as a liability, a cost or curse. It took her breath away. It hurt her deeply. She struggles still with the complicated sense of bringing down the value of one's own home, just by being.

I grew up in a neighbourhood that was 'blockbusted'. I was around nine when it happened. Our family had been the only Black family in the area for sixty years. When another Black family moved in, an alarm went off within white homes, and within a year and a half, literally all the friends I had grown up with – and with whom my mother had grown up – had disappeared. It was wrenching, and among the most emotionally unsettling experiences of my life. As an adult, however, I have only recently begun to think of the emotional toll on those who fled. The race-baiting of realtors who went door-to-door and preyed on the emotional vulnerabilities of our first- and second-generation immigrant neighbours from Ireland, Italy, Germany and Russia. They had fled pogroms and hunger and serfdom. I remember sitting on the front porch of my friends' homes while realtors told their parents that they would lose everything they had unless they packed up and got out before everything 'turned'.

President Trump has framed many of his 2020 campaign ads in terms that stoke very similar fears. In advance of the election, he revoked an anti-discrimination law guaranteeing fairness in housing with the tweeted reassurance that, 'People fight all of their lives to get into the suburbs and have a beautiful home. There will be no more low-income housing forced into the suburbs ... Enjoy your life, ladies and gentlemen.' In another tweet addressed to 'the Suburban Housewives of America' he warned 'Biden will destroy your neighborhood and your American Dream'.

Yet I don't remember those urgently departing white neighbours as bad people. They served me Kool-Aid and cookies and gave me birthday gifts. We wandered in and out of each other's homes, did homework together, borrowed toys, played all day in each other's back yards. It was a safe and peaceful environment. But I am struck by how easily their genuine friendliness was transformed by the simple threat of an entirely imaginary 'enemy' invasion. Their curiosity about new neighbours was entirely eclipsed by a fear so deep I could not begin to grasp it as a child. Their *lives depended* on 'getting away' as one little girl told me the day before the moving truck pulled up. They never said goodbye. They moved to a suburb that is still nearly all-white. Only in watching the fear-mongering talents of the Trump administration have I begun to consider how frightened those families must have been long before the realtors came calling. They upended everything in their lives upon a threat crafted, intentionally or not, to echo something like 'The Cossacks are coming! Run now!' That racialized fragility, as Robin

DiAngelo has described it,[9] is one of the entangled ways that the legacy of white supremacy plays itself forward through the family narratives of those whose ancestors were not directly associated with slavery.[10] Racism is a viral fantasy that consumes histories, redirects empathy, consolidates fear. It erodes our ability to connect in sustained ways. We cannot possibly learn to be neighbours if our inner precariousness is always whispering that it might be time to flee.

This quiet but hugely significant segregation redounds through American schools and workplaces and political expectations. Therefore, it should be no surprise that, when we arrive at college or university and suddenly have to deal with a roommate of a different race, subliminal anxiety spills over in all kinds of encounters. Sometimes it drives people into fraternities or sororities that consciously or unconsciously segregate themselves racially, though we're normally too polite to put it in such terms. Instead, we say it's by interest group or class or aesthetic, who's 'hot' or who likes golf or skiing, whose parents know whom – as though those categories were not themselves raced and gendered and reflective of class. The truth spills out when photos of frat parties in blackface percolate into yearbooks or onto the internet.

Race, gender, ethnicity, mother tongue, cultural perspective – all these things condition how we interact with each other, what we experience in encounters with salespeople, with teachers, or with police. It affects our opportunities in the job market or the willingness of doctors to touch our bodies in healing ways; whether, when I shake your hand, I am greeted as a blank slate to be discovered and learned about, or whether others think they already know me because my existence is over-determined by narratives of suspicion. Some of this is at the base of our so-called culture wars, the campus clashes, our chalked-up encounters. But perhaps it's really important for all of us to arm ourselves with big boxes of Kleenex – rather than rifles – and buckets of patience so we can weep and shout and gnash our teeth, but not give up. We must be kinder to one another, and relatively forgiving when we weep and gnash our teeth and say the wrong thing. We are all learning. We are always all learning. These encounters are bound to be painful when we are raised in multiple different worlds.

Without committed engagement, the American civil rights movement's aspiration to the constitutional right of 'public accommodation' will remain compromised. In our courts we fight about whether a baker has to serve gays; or whether a hospital can discriminate against non-Catholics; or whether we have to serve food to someone who is of a different political party; or whether an employer can compel polyglots to speak English only. As a society, we are increasingly defined by our profound fear of non-conformity where the steady creep of walls against any measure of the unknown feels like good sense. Gated communities. More prisons than anyplace on the planet. The thin blue line. The glass ceiling. The country club. The athletic club. Kindergartens and middle schools that have more hoop-jumping entrance requirements than Homeland Security. Most Americans are further cocooned by speaking only one language – and even disparage those who are fluent in anything but English – when in a global economy we really all should be learning three or four languages in order to survive. Within our little walled circles we may feel safer or better, but we don't know the world beyond those walls. And in a world of global diaspora and increasingly porous need, it might be better to start thinking outside the literal and metaphoric box.

V. 'The Eyes of the Jungle'

'I can't think about that right now.
If I do, I'll go crazy.'[1]

We don't like to talk about our history; we don't like our misperceptions to be challenged. And so we live with hypocrisy and blatant double standards. When one thinks of the culture wars, one must recall that one of the most hotly contested issues of the last twenty years has been the question of freedom of speech. When university students of colour have protested the use of ethnic slurs, they are routinely met with robust cries of 'censorship'. Yet it is rare that what goes on in universities actually constitutes legal censorship. After all, the First Amendment to the US Constitution only protects Americans from government censorship; jurisprudentially it is defined as 'prior restraint' by an empowered authority, usually the government. As unpleasant and wrong-headed as it may be, it does not generally encompass campus fracas in which angry, hurt, or crying students tell each other to shut up.

The true power of censorship is the chilling effect on political systems, of being surveilled and knowing you'll be punished by state action for expressing views that are not in accord with state authority. Censorship is when politicians decide that union membership is 'communist' and communism is conflated with treason, as Senator Joseph McCarthy did. Censorship is when you express sympathy with #BlackLivesMatter, or take a knee, or prosecute an officer for excessive force, and, in retaliation, the police department decides it's not going to respond to your phone calls for help in an emergency.[2] Censorship is when football players who wish to express a political opinion by assuming a prayerful position – who literally get down on their knees in a posture of peace – are taunted by the President of the United States with calls that they be summarily fired.[3] Censorship is when government has the power to read your emails and secretly interview your neighbours and employer and forbid them to say anything to you about it, as the USA Patriot Act putatively allows.[4] We should be at least as worried about that as we are about whether sophomoric shouting matches, literally among college sophomores, constitute anything like the same.

Censorship is also voter suppression. And censorship is when the chief executive recasts the free press – the very embodiment of the First Amendment and public accountability – as 'the enemy of the people'.[5] Censorship is when a president decides to punish anyone who asks him a tough question by banning them from the White House press corps.[6]

The American Constitution enshrines freedom of speech, worship and publication as central in the rich tradition of Anglo-American jurisprudence. As a cultural matter, however, freedom of expression carries symbolism that exceeds legal discourse or political libertarianism; it has become a very anxiety-provoking concept at the center of our culture wars. The First Amendment is rather too often invoked as a right to spew invective or to set up conversational roadblocks, as in 'I have my right to call you a rapist parasite, so you shut up about it.' I worry, moreover, about the degree to which having really passionate exchange is sometimes re-described as censorship. I worry that the rhetorical understanding of concepts like disturbing the peace, harassment, defamation, hate speech, humor, mockery, shaming, taunting, humiliation and sadism is lost or treated as though beside the point as we say over and over, *it's just freedom of speech*. And if you chafe at my right to shout you down in the middle of Fifth Avenue, then you're censoring me.

This is very reductive.

As a lawyer, I worry particularly about the erosion of due process, that ritual space in which the right to speak holds hands with the right to be heard. Due process is a catechism of courtesy, a clearing of time to listen to one another's stories and to think about them. As flawed as this may often be in practice, the adherence to a system of stopping to think before we banish or imprison or execute is an important commitment, an attempt at patience and accountability. A hearing is not just a badge of citizenship, it is – or ought to be – a basic human right. But a hearing requires space, rules of exchange, and consensus about who says what and in what order. And hearing one another usually works best with evidentiary limits: in courtrooms, at least, the rules worked out over centuries exclude what's irrelevant or too inflammatory or too unreliable as hearsay. In a world driven by social media that shreds those norms in every sphere, we fall prey to thoughtless speed, contagious emotional extremes, and anonymously generated rumour.

It's not just the corrosion of having every American institution – from A to Z – made suspect by the label 'fake, fake and more fake'.[7] Momentous global events – like war or climate change – aren't being taken very seriously, because somehow nothing feels real. This is different from fake. If we look at the world as unreal, we are also putting it at a distance. Unreality is quieter than alleging that everyone's lying or out to get you. Unreality is a kind of ignoring; it is a self-imposed ignorance. It does not engage our capacity to envision futures, of freedom or fulfilment. What will it take to wake us in a world when so many alarms are clanging? Why is it so seductive to roll over and pull that pillow back over our heads?

The unreality of one another's experience allows us to live in parallel universes. We shut each other out. And this makes it easier to experience someone else's expressive rights and integrity as inherently challenging to one's own.[8]

'Prior restraint' used to be a fairly well-defined concept, particularly in the area of First Amendment jurisprudence. At least in the abstract, it is generally accepted that we do not punish ideas – what someone reads or says or thinks – unless those ideas threaten to depart the realm of mere ideas, becoming a 'clear and present danger'. There are two significant forces that are converging to compromise that settled law, both in the US and abroad. The first is the rise of global fear about terrorism. The second is, again, the enormously complex communicative power of the internet.

Many of us have spent the last few decades of the academic culture wars debating the definition of dangerous speech. Those debates have been mostly focused on hate-filled tracts like *Mein Kampf* or *The Turner Diaries*, or on the governance of the dark web and internet trolls, or on the power of suggestive images like Sarah Palin's placement of rifle cross-hairs over the faces of her political opponents.[9] In the US, these debates have rarely budged beyond sunny bromides about how hate speech must be met with more speech – even as we have also arrived at a weird kind of equivalent rhetorical standoff between the First and Second Amendments, in which mass murder must be met by arming more 'good guys' with 'more guns'.[10]

This leads me to the matter of creating safe spaces, an enterprise that is often mocked as infantilizing or silly or coddling. But I take the issue seriously – as an injunction to carefully examine the role of alcohol, guns and untreated mental illness, as well as the cultural pathologies of racism and sexism or other -isms. We all deserve a quiet place in which to think, learn, teach, and explore ideas. In a world that increasingly imagines itself under siege, however, we seem to be creating not rooms of our own but bunkers against others: private walled spaces that divide us into smaller and smaller boxes rather than seeking any modicum of public accommodation. We are failing in thinking about how we can share public geographies, how we can share in ways that permit us to co-exist mutually, in the enjoyment of each other's company – fearlessly and tolerantly, compassionately and forgivingly.

In university settings, we have brought somewhat bureaucratic solutions to bear, writing contracts to consent to have sex, or warning each other when we're going to bring up a subject that's likely to evoke traumatic stress in our classmates. After all, we live in a society with so much gunfire and rape and violence that a whole lot of us do indeed have PTSD. But it requires some broad conceptual redefinition to really comprehend what's at stake: first some sharing of and consideration of the deep history of each other's experience; and second, some recognition of how treating these problems as a kind of private property hobbles citizenship and disenfranchises us all in very insidious ways.

The question of speech as imminently threatening or incendiary is particularly complicated in the American context, where the right to bear arms has been deemed an expansive individual right.[11] If the massive gun rights rally in Richmond, Virginia, is frightening to some of us for its size, intimate encounters with open-carry are no less unsettling. Consider the situation of Professor Steven Weinberg, a Nobel Prize-winning physicist at the University of Texas at Austin. He closed his seminars to anyone carrying a firearm, fearing that guns in the classroom chill discussion. For this, he became vulnerable to lawsuit under Texas's 'campus carry' law, which permits individuals to carry concealed handguns on campuses and into classrooms.[12]

Meanwhile, clever students staged demonstrations on the Austin campus pitting 'campus carry' up against another Texas law that forbids individuals from displaying or distributing obscene materials.[13] Thousands of students came together to protest guns on campus by attaching 'gigantic swinging dildos' to their backpacks. The logic was summed up thus: 'You're carrying a gun to class? Yeah, well I'm carrying a HUGE DILDO.' Dildos are, as organizer Jessica Jin pointed out, 'just about as effective at protecting us from sociopathic shooters, but much safer for recreational play'.[14] A veritable jouissance of expressive freedom may be found at #CocksNotGlocks.

If open-carry laws are attractive to many self-styled citizen-soldiers for their projected force-field of 'don't tread on me', there is no less 'get out of my face' aggression conveyed with the ubiquitous, ritualized, accidentally-on-purpose donning of blackface as 'just free speech'. 'Where did this come from?' we ask ourselves as each new blackface scandal emerges like an eternal game of political whack-a-mole. But there is little that is new under the sun; and the stickiness of internet memes is often related to their sensed familiarity, rooted in much deeper emotional histories. Every other day it seems there's something: an entire fraternity house in blackface.[15] Or the Canadian Prime Minister Justin Trudeau, in blackface and a turban.[16] In February, 2019, the high-end fashion label Gucci kicked off Black History Month with the debut of an $890 black balaclava with big red knit lips encircling the mouth.[17] The luxury coat manufacturer Moncler apologized after mass-producing a heavily allusive line of clothing emblazoned with loud images of blackfaced 'golliwogs'[18] – as has Prada.[19] In

2019, Virginia's Attorney General, Mark Herring admitted donning blackface at a frat party when he was a student.[20] And a photo taken in 2015 at Covington Catholic High School in Kentucky captured crowds of students, many in full blackface and body paint, taunting African American basketball players from a visiting school.[21]

As the *Washington Post* critic Robin Givhan has written, none of this was done by 'elementary school children with a tenuous grasp on American history' – or European colonial history for that matter – it is done by those who must know better: teens, adults and full-scale multinational corporate conglomerates.[22] 'Whether some sleek photograph in a fashion magazine or a grainy one in an Eastern Virginia Medical School yearbook, it's all the same. Blackface gets to the discomforting core of how black people are seen by the broader culture and how some white people see themselves.'[23]

How indeed. Why is this not ancient history rather than a resurgent pattern of behaviour? What is it that white people who don blackface see in themselves when doing so? 'School spirit', is how officials defended it at Covington Catholic High School. (It was also 'school spirit' that supposedly accounted for the rowdy chorus of 'tomahawk chops' recorded on the Washington Mall during a face-off between a laughing horde of white Covington students and an indigenous drummer, Omaha elder Nathan Phillips.[24])

Blackface is widely dismissed by those who perform it as 'a joke'. But if this is humour, it is a very aggressive form of humour. Over and over, this 'play' is met with loud public protest, unequivocally condemned by us Black people whose faces are played upon. Yet on and on it goes, too often, too repetitively, always just an 'unfortunate', 'momentary' lapse of judgement. There's a strong undercurrent of defiance, an aggression whose subtext is 'piss off – just try and make me stop'. It reminds me of a version of the Confederate flag that I saw for sale at a roadside stand in rural Washington state: a large black assault weapon printed across the flag, and under that the words: 'Come And Take It'. There is something like that threat in the gleeful taunting, in the persistent, insistent claim that blackface is 'unintentional', unmeant racism.

'For some people,' observes Robin Givhan, 'the idea of dressing up in blackface is just another form of drag.' And while drag can be subversive, ironic, liberating and gender-bending, blackface is 'more than drag [...] It's painful, shared history of course. But it's also the horrible present. And it's a likely part of a crummy future. Blackface is denial and ignorance. It's narcissism, willfulness and disdain.' As Givhan summarizes, 'Racism is not measured by how you treat the person-of-color you know, but by how you treat the ones you don't. It's not measured by your affection for the singular black person but your respect for black people in general.'[25]

In a sense, blackface operates as a kind of surveillance. It gestures at a phenotype that may be mocked; it makes theatre of Black defilement while passing as 'jocular' white (mostly male) bonding. It is a ritual with near-magical consequence.

VI. 'The Great Heart'

'[A]pologies, once postponed, become harder and harder to make, and finally impossible.'[1]

The word neighbour comes from the Old English word 'neahgebur' meaning 'near landman' – an adjacent farmer, a contiguous tiller of the same scape. If good fences make good neighbours, it helps to think of neighbourliness as an equal knowing of a particular space. Gebur also means peasant, although given modern inflections, it helps to think of that much as 'countryman'. Yet 'gebur' is also the root of the modern word 'boor' (as in boorish), perhaps pointing to the underlying limits of propinquity – the too-nearness, the risks of intimacy's transgressions. And, just as the concepts of host and hostile share the same etymology, so the notion of neighbourliness and boorishness are wrapped together at the root.

Being seen as 'out of place' is dangerously dehumanizing, as Mary Douglas observed; one risks being made dirty, bestial, 'less than'.[2] Thus, the assignment of belonging or dispossession is an enormously powerful incantation – it functions like the rigid hierarchies of caste, particularly when asserted in the name of great institutional police power.[3] 'They look so innocent. They're not innocent,' says President Donald Trump, when speaking of children torn from their parents at the border.[4] 'These aren't people' is how he describes adolescents about whom he knows nothing but their nationality.[5] Immigrants 'are animals, and we're taking them out of the country at a level and a rate that's never happened before,' adds Trump.[6] Their children will be put in 'foster care or whatever', according to the then White House Chief of Staff, General John Kelly.[7]

The inability to see in another even the potential for neighbourliness is one kind of wall. This disconnect allows us to more easily deprive that other of care, respect, regard and human rights. It is a quiet act of war to say, for example, that this or that human child is beyond the pale of 'our' civilization. And yet it seems almost painless, to paint children as predators, as we do juveniles – particularly Black juveniles – in America's school-to-prison pipeline. From 2013 to 2018, at least 30,467 children under the age of 10 were arrested in the United States, some as young as six and some for misbehaviour like hiding in the classroom, having a tantrum, or refusing to go to the principal's office.[8] Thirty-four

American states have no minimum age for delinquency. And twenty-four states have no minimum age for transferring juvenile cases to adult criminal courts.

The practice of handcuffing and jailing even very young children has been extended to the largely Central American youth now detained by Border and Customs Patrol. But sealing young children, even babies, away in cages and in concentration camps, and separating them from their parents indefinitely is a form of genocide. We must be clear about this: it is a grave violation of human rights because it is a slow way of killing them. And although numbers are extremely hard to come by, best estimates indicate that US border officials apprehended more than 76,000 unaccompanied minors in 2019 alone.[9] There are at least 15,000 migrant children in US border detention.[10] In 2018, at least 2,700 of those were separated from parents or family while in detention; although recent reports from the Department of Health and Human Services indicate with alarming vagueness and lack of accountability that 'thousands more' could be as well.[11]

Some of these children have been confined in Brownsville, Texas, in what was once a Walmart store. 'Casa Padre' is its inspired and ironic new name, and nearly 1,500 boys under the age of 18 are housed there. In pictures of the entrance hallway one can see a huge graffito of Donald Trump's head, oddly disembodied, looming larger than a minuscule image of the White House, above which he floats, godlike, in the sky. The mural includes a quote from Trump's book, *The Art of the Deal*: 'Sometimes by losing a battle you find a new way to win the war.'[12]

There is little in constitutional or human rights law to justify this barbarity, but some have turned to what they seem to think is God's law.[13] When put on the defensive about child separations, the former Attorney General Jeff Sessions invoked the Pauline Epistle of Romans 13, which reads:

> Let everyone be subject to the governing authorities, for there is no authority except that which God has established. The authorities that exist have been established by God. Consequently, whoever rebels against the authority is rebelling against what God has instituted, and those who do so will bring judgment on themselves. For rulers hold no terror for those who do right, but for those who do wrong. Do you want to be free from fear of the one in authority? Then do what is right and you will be commended. For the one in authority is God's servant for your good. But if you do wrong, be afraid, for rulers do not bear the sword for no reason. They are God's servants, agents of wrath to bring punishment on the wrongdoer. Therefore, it

is necessary to submit to the authorities, not only because of possible punishment but also as a matter of conscience.

Attorney General Jefferson Beauregard Sessions, III, whose very name summons two of the most notorious slaveholders and officials of the Confederate States of America – Jefferson Davis and P. G. T. Beauregard – was using a feint common in the antebellum South, where Romans 13 was frequently invoked to justify the Fugitive Slave Act, by which slaves who had run to freedom in the north were captured and returned. It is God's law, divine will, it was said then as it is said now. It's just the 'natural' order of things – not a policy dreamed up by the President and enacted at his command – that compels government agents, masters, and other authorities to treat slaves, immigrants and livestock like inventory.

Throughout the antebellum period, slavery hardened Americans to the terror and grief of a trade that put human beings on the auction block, took babies from their mothers and sold them to strangers. After the Civil War, the American Eugenics Movement took up the mantle as a potent purveyor of dehumanizing notions.[14] During the early part of the twentieth century, juvenile reform policies encouraged the removal of children from people deemed unfit, 'feeble-minded', 'promiscuous', or epileptic.[15] These parents were disproportionately Irish immigrants, people of colour, or unmarried women.[16] Policy-makers throughout the country championed programmes of 'social hygiene' that led not only to the removal of 'defective' Black children from their equally 'defective' parents, but also to the confinement of those children in adult prisons.[17] Until recently, states sterilized thousands of women – and some men – for reasons that included lightening the perceived tax burden of those deemed the 'undeserving' poor, those not deemed refined enough to fit through the sieve-like conception of civilization.[18] Today, our policies continue this indifference through the cruelties of the school-to-prison pipeline, arresting even 6-year-olds[19] and increasingly militarizing the interiors of public schools.[20]

Indeed, we seem to have learned nothing from the rampant sadness and alcoholism that plagues American Indian reservations to this day, and which is directly related to the thousands of children who were taken from the care of their parents, who lost their mother tongues, and who were boarded at schools that 'Christianized' them with neglect, beatings and sexual abuse.[21] Today's detention centres at the southern border don't even pretend to be schools. Many of the children speak Mayan or other indigenous dialects for which there are few translators. They endure the isolation of having no one who can understand them even in health emergencies. Moreover, the levels of sexual and other physical abuse are staggering. Between 2014 and 2018, there have been 4,556 allegations of sexual assault or sexual harassment of separated and detained minors: According to a Justice Department report, 'The records [...] detailed allegations that adult staff members had harassed and assaulted children, including fondling and kissing minors, watching them as they showered and raping them. They also included cases of suspected abuse of children by other minors.'[22]

The persistence of such violations rely on very old rationalizations: certain classes of human beings are not 'really' human; they do not feel pain to the same degree as 'more civilized' classes; these 'others' are incorrigibly predisposed to prevarication (or 'acting', as conservative pundit Ann Coulter recently dismissed the images of bereft immigrant toddlers[23]). Above all, 'they' are always kept at a distance. This 'they'-making obliterates due process, equal protection and individual justice. It justifies racial and ethnic profiling, as when rationalizing the exclusion of Chinese Americans,[24] the internment of Japanese Americans[25] and the mass incarceration of African Americans.[26] Indeed, President Trump has said repeatedly he thinks it's 'common sense' to punish in the plural: '[Y]ou have to take out their families,' he has said of those he deems terrorists, thus rendering extended communities of innocents mere instruments of vengeance.[27]

The United States government argues that the deliberate separation of parents and children will serve as a disincentive to others seeking to cross the border. This alone is a crime against humanity. The United States is the only member of the United Nations that has not ratified the Convention on the Rights of the Child. Article 2 of that convention specifically prohibits punishing or discriminating against a child 'on the basis of the status, activities, expressed opinions, or beliefs of the child's parents, legal guardians, or family members'. Article 5 requires that 'States Parties shall respect the responsibilities, rights and duties of parents or, where applicable, the members of the extended family or community as provided for by local custom, legal guardians or other persons legally responsible for the child, to provide, in a manner consistent with the evolving capacities of the child, appropriate direction and guidance in the exercise by the child of the rights recognised in the present Convention.' Article 8 provides that children have a right to their identity 'including nationality, name and family relations'. Article 9 ensures that 'States Parties shall ensure that a child shall not be separated from his or her parents against their will, except when competent authorities subject to judicial review determine, in accordance with applicable law and procedures, that such separation is necessary for the best interests of the child', and Article 21 ensures that the adoption system operates in the best interests of the child.

The reason the United Nations has a convention for protection for the rights of children is that the scientific evidence solidly proves that children subjected to the trauma of separation from loved ones during the crucial early years of development suffer catastrophic damage to the very architecture of their brains. We know this from the horrific clarity that narratives of family separations in Nazi concentration camps provided.[28] We know this based on studies of children who were abandoned in Romanian orphanages during the 1980s and early 1990s who were found to have grown up with less cerebral white and grey matter than their peers raised by even not-so-perfect parents. We know this from the American foster-care system which is deeply scarring, even when children are separated from their families to protect them from danger. Forty to fifty per cent of children who age-out of foster care become homeless within eighteen months.[29] Fully half of America's homeless population were foster children at some point.[30]

It is in these ways that ideas honed in slavery – of otherness, of boorishness, of the inferior humanity of thy neighbour – have continued to travel through American society so long after the Emancipation Proclamation.

We understand all these things, and yet we do not scrutinize this manufactured tragedy as it unfolds. The detention camps on the border with Mexico are off-limits to the public. Even members of Congress have been denied entry without two weeks' notice – and the locations of many of the detention centres have been withheld, making them hard to inspect or hold accountable.[31]

When the First Lady Melania Trump visited one of the children's detention centres in Texas, she wore a coat emblazoned with the words 'I really don't care, Do U?' (The coat was manufactured by Zara, an Italian company previously under fire for producing a miniskirt with the alt-right symbol of Pepe the Frog emblazoned on it, a purse with a swastika and a prison-striped T-shirt with a yellow star affixed to it.) Trump says she wore the coat 'for the people and for the left-wing media who are criticizing me. And I want to show them that I don't care.'[32] Accepting this as true, the language is nevertheless chillingly similar to the slogan of Benito Mussolini's Stormtroopers, the *arditi*, or so-called blackshirts.[33] '*Me ne frego/Me ne frego/Me ne Frego e il nostro motto*' is a line from the anthem of Mussolini's National Fascist Party. It translates as 'I don't care/I don't care/I don't care is our motto.' While the slogan and the party have been outlawed in Italy, the phrase '*Me ne frego*' has enjoyed a resurgence among European fascists and neo-Nazis. Its clearest ideological inheritor is Casa Pound (named for Ezra Pound), led by Gianluca Iannone (who has '*Me ne frego*' tatooed on his neck).[34] To this day, that slogan is to be found on T-shirts and banners throughout Italy and Eastern Europe; and there is a healthy commerce in badges, patches and pins available on Amazon. Moreover, Melania Trump, who claims to speak Italian,[35] was born in Nova Mesta, a city in a part of Slovenia that borders Italy, in the canton of Ljubljana, which was annexed by Fascist Italy during World War II, and subjected to Mussolini's radical plan for 'Italianization' of the 'inferior and barbaric' Slavic 'races'. Ljubljana today is home to much of Slovenia's furthest antisemitic and homophobic right-wing organizations who still embrace Mussolini's motto.[36] It seems almost inconceivable that our First Lady would not be aware of this resonance.

The question remains unanswered: Does a coat speak? What does it signify? We go about our daily business, not looking because we do not want to know. We pass the abandoned Walmart, this parking lot for disposable despair, this factory for future fury. And we quarantine this all-American banality of evil as the problem of 'someone else's babies', whose torture we disown.

VII. 'Vengeance Is Mine'

'She remembered her hot joy in shooting the
marauding Yankee. Violent blood was in them all,
perilously close to the surface, lurking just beneath
the kindly courteous exteriors. All of them, all the
men she knew, even the drowsy-eyed Ashley and
fidgety old Frank, were like that underneath –
murderous, violent if the need arose. Even Rhett,
conscienceless scamp that he was, had killed a man
for being "uppity to a lady".'[1]

In March of 2019, President Donald Trump issued an
executive order to 'protect' speech on college campuses.[2]
When asked about what the order was meant to
accomplish that the First Amendment didn't already
provide, the President gave an oddly wandering reply
that seemed to include an off-the-cuff threat: 'I can tell
you, I have the support of the police, the support of the
military, the support of the Bikers for Trump – I have the
tough people, but they don't play it tough until they go

to a certain point, and then it would be very bad, very bad.'[3]

If Trump's threat of force-by-biker-gangs sounded inconsistent with his mandate of free speech, the backdrop against which he spoke was even more remarkable. The news that week was filled with reports that the Venezuelan President Nicolás Maduro had been deploying armed motorcycle gangs as extrajudicial enforcers in his country.[4] (By the same token, Vladimir Putin's fondness for the paramilitary bikers known as the Night Wolves is notorious.[5]) Trump's statement also came just days before a sitting member of Congress – yes, Representative Steve King again – hypothesized so nostalgically about 'another civil war' in the United States: 'One side has about 8 trillion bullets, while the other side doesn't know which bathroom to use ... Wonder who would win.'[6] Again, an alarming image of our polity divided between armed and unarmed, right and left, the tough and those who didn't see it coming.

Most glaringly, Trump bragged about his de facto backup crew just days before a heavily armed gunman killed fifty Muslims in New Zealand and cited the US president as a 'symbol of renewed white identity'[7] (albeit just 'one time', as the presidential aide Kellyanne Conway noted helpfully[8]). Obviously, a politician's words don't necessarily make him liable for the acts of his admirers. But it is not even necessary here to prove a direct link between Trump's speech and the violence it inspires. It is just as worrying that there is an American president who so relentlessly dehumanizes, infantilizes, hypersexualizes, pathologizes and criminalizes. Trump is not Hitler, but the rhetoric he employs isn't that far off. Hitler wrote that Jews were a 'poison' to national bodies, causing 'a ferment of decomposition' among peoples and races that renders them, in the broader sense, 'a dissolver of human culture'.[9] Trump and many of his appointees have reinvigorated such sentiments with caustic new life, applying them to everyone from Mexicans to Muslims to Democrats to dead war heroes: low-IQ, lowlife, parasitic, worst-of-the-worst, scummy, wussy, disgraceful, ugly, fat-faced, coddled, vicious, animal, raping, drug-dealing, a bad-very-bad subhuman invasion. Latin American migrants are an actual 'infestation', according to the President of the United States.[10]

The *Washington Post* recently published statistics showing that counties that hosted Trump rallies in 2016 saw a 226 per cent increase in hate crimes over comparable counties that did not host a Trump rally. While direct causal relationship is impossible to prove, 'It is hard to discount a "Trump effect" when a considerable number of these reported hate crimes reference Trump,' the story noted.[11] The FBI's Universal Crime Report showed a 17 per cent rise in hate crimes in 2017.

Recently, the actor Liam Neeson confessed that he had once felt the urge to go out and kill a 'black bastard' after an unnamed friend had been raped.[12] His confession to an interviewer included these words:

> I asked, did she know who it was? No. What color were they? She said it was a black person. I went up and down areas with a cosh, hoping I'd be approached by somebody – I'm ashamed to say that – and I did it for maybe a week, hoping some black bastard would come out of a pub and have a go at me about something, you know? So that I could kill him.[13]

This description is astonishing for many reasons, but at the same time, it contains many of the more quotidian elements of casual racism. It contains the unvarnished ease of reductive representation, by which one 'black bastard' becomes any Black person at all.

Neeson blamed this thought process on the blindness that descends in rage, on the seductions of fear and vulnerability. I can understand that. It's what trauma does – it's a distortion of the senses. You are injured or a loved one is – you are tempted to re-enact the injury, sometimes without full capacity to rein in the impulse or to make granular distinctions or to engage the critical capacity to realize that this one is not like that other.

Luckily Neeson did not act. Luckily he now knows it was the irrational heat of vigilantism. He says he's ashamed, which is also commendable. But the story is nonetheless disturbing.

By his own account, the first thing he asked his friend was 'What colour was he?' So the association between 'I was raped' and *colour* was a habit of thought that long preceded the rape. That particular linkage is yet another cultural tailwind of the long history of blackface.[14] It was not until the early twentieth century that white performers began to darken their faces. While the use of cork, ash and boot polish to darken the faces of comedians dates back to the 1800s, in vaudeville and in stylized dances like the cakewalk, it was mostly Black performers who did it. (Bert Williams is perhaps the earliest and best known of these whose work is captured on film.) It was comedic, demeaning perhaps, but in the fashion of *Amos 'n' Andy*:[15] full of exaggerated emotions and gestural silliness, infantilizing but not inherently *criminalized*.

The big shift came with *Birth of a Nation*, most notably when the white actor, Walter Long, donned blackface makeup to play Gus, the villainous anti-hero and 'renegade negro', whose brutal assault on white women coalesces the Klan to deadly revenge. (All the supposedly Black characters in that film were played by white men painted black.) The story makes the fate of history depend on the aggressive assertion not merely of white supremacy but upon Black inferiority and the suppression of even the slightest political power to which Black people might aspire. In *Birth of a Nation*, the Ku Klux Klan is the heroic force; Black men the looming danger. Its influence became so outsized in succeeding years and the use of blackface so conjoined with threat, lynching and degradation of Black humanity, that blackface ceased being simply comedic or inane; it became a white vehicle for expressing racialized contempt. Just beneath the skin of that contempt was the figuration of Black men as rapists and fomenters of slave rebellion. (This exaggerated fear of Black rape was perhaps also the complexly psychoanalytic, barely repressed, performative echo of white slaveholders' unbridled use of Black women for sexual release, as well as for slave breeding.) In any event, *Birth of a Nation*'s enormous popularity made it one of the most powerful pieces of propaganda ever to visit the screen, a tribute to the vast new technological impact of cinema.

Liam Neeson's instant association of rape and colour is a product of that history and of that ideation. It certainly wasn't the product of his specific lived reality – Neeson was in Ireland at the time. He apparently searched for a whole week without coming across any Blacks to kill.

The question this raises is: what would he have done if his friend had said her assailant were white? Would he have gone down to the local bar looking for white men to kill? Would he have killed himself? I think there's little chance he would have stayed at such a broad category – he'd probably have taken a minute to ask what the man looked like: was he short or tall, old or young, did he have a beard, or an accent, or a scar, or a limp.[16]

I have written before about a conversation I had years ago with two white friends one of whom described going to the hospital for an obstetrical procedure of some sort and finding herself sharing a room with a 16-year-old girl who was pregnant. 'Was she Black?' asked the other friend. I was struck by the implied assumption that white teenagers wouldn't get themselves knocked up; or that it would be only Black teens who get pregnant at such a young age. It was presumptuous, not asking any other question when there were so many other questions one might have thought would come first: what were her circumstances, where was her family, had she wanted to become pregnant or was it that she did not have access to birth control. Instead – the first question is too often all about colour. *If it's a bad thing, it must be a Black thing.*

'But she *was* Black!' protested the first friend. And that's where the conversation always gets stuck in self-fulfilling prophecy and carelessly applied proxies. Prejudice is prejudgement made true: if we start out by labelling a person or thing as less valuable or more dangerous, the ensuing neglect, avoidance and stigma leads to more poverty, less access to goods and fewer services including employment opportunity, good schooling and proper health care. Racism rationalizes its irrationality with circular thinking: the jumbling of time and causation, of singular and plural.

This habit of reading the world is just that: habit. But it's not easy to break habits or change culture. As the poet Claudia Rankine has observed, 'The world is wrong. You can't put the past behind you. It's buried in you; it's turned your flesh into its own cupboard.'[17]

The philosopher Lynne Tirrell has written about toxic speech in the contexts of Nazi demagoguery and the Rwandan genocide.[18] Speaking about the dehumanizing images deployed in the Rwandan genocide, she observes that boys 'learn how to kill a snake with a machete, and so when Tutsi were called snakes, the Hutu militia knew exactly how to attack'.[19] She notes that the bipolar division into 'us and them' is an especially efficient action-engendering device in the creation of bunkered populations. She casts it as a public-health problem in which hateful phrases spread and can be tracked according to predictive patterns that 'divide groups, make people think the group division is natural', and encourage the use of 'derogatory terms to refer to the group you plan to eliminate, especially terms that have action-engendering power'.[20] Words that are 'action-engendering' – that move people to act – are sometimes understood as imperatives or as having institutional heft. They are the bridge from purely linguistic descriptions to the non-linguistic behaviours that such terms license or permit.

Indeed, of all the lines from Liam Neeson's interview professing his desire to kill a Black man, there was one mostly under-reported throw-away that I found profoundly unsettling, particularly in light of Tirrell's warning about the potential of 'action-engendering' speech. Neeson described his character's need for violent revenge in the film *Cold Pursuit*:

> I think audience members live to see that. They can kind of live vicariously through it. People say 'Yeah, but violence in films makes people want to go out and kill people.' I don't believe that at all. I think the average moviegoer thinks, 'Yeah, punch him. Punch him.' And they get a satisfaction out of seeing somebody else enact it, and they leave the theater and they feel satiated in some way.

I fear there is just such a vicarious 'punch him' 'satisfaction' in President Trump's polarized vision of American destiny: Republicans versus Democrats, right versus left, real versus fake, good versus bad, 'our people' versus the rest. For all his professed devotion to the notion of free speech, Trump has consistently expressed the wish to shut up and put down those whom he deems not among 'my people'. At a Michigan rally, he urged security guards to remove a protester with these words: 'Get him out. Try not to hurt him. If you do, I'll defend you in court ... Are Trump rallies the most fun? We're having a good time.'[21] When a protester heckled him at a gathering in Las Vegas, Trump declared: 'I'd like to punch him in the face.'[22] The President even offered to pay the legal fees for one of his supporters, John McGraw, who sucker-punched a Black heckler and then told an *Inside Edition* crew that 'we might have to kill him' if he saw the protester again. McGraw, Trump purred, 'obviously loves the country'.[23]

It ought to vex us, the question of how violence might be rehearsed; and whether 'vicarious' enjoyment in deadly display might eventually leave the confines of theatre and become projected beyond Neeson's neat realm of the imaginary. Hitler described the bonding effects of mass meetings as essential for 'esprit de corps'. He wrote in *Mein Kampf*: 'When from his little workshop or big factory, in which he feels very small, [the ordinary man] steps for the first time into a mass meeting and has thousands and thousands of people of the same opinion around him [...] when the visible success and agreement of thousands confirm to him the rightness of the new doctrine and for the first time arouse doubt in the truth of his previous conviction – then he himself has succumbed to the magic influence of what we designate as 'mass suggestion'.[24]

We must fear any leader who manipulates his power by tossing the red meat of insult to rouse armed warriors to his side. Even idle or careless incitement from those who also command armies carries the weight of constant threat, for such speech may be construed as imperative. Which of 'us' will follow that command?

VIII. 'The Fiery Cross'

'I want the old days back again and they'll
never come back, and I am haunted by the
memory of them and of the world falling about
my ears.'[1]

Some years ago I was invited to speak at Cambridge University, and I was fortunate enough to be put up in the Rylands Suite. It is a lovely little set of rooms once occupied by thespian and Bloomsbury member George Rylands.[2] It was here Rylands invited Virginia Woolf for lunch in the 1920s. And it was on this visit, during luncheon at King's College, Cambridge, that Woolf found inspiration for *A Room of One's Own*, in which she summarizes her experience of being told that she could not walk on the same path with the men of the college, and her resultant sense of 'out of place-ness'.[3] The book is Woolf's meditation not merely upon the conditions necessary for creative expression, but also the preconditions necessary for women's autonomy and safety.

The Rylands Suite is a really pretty space. There are murals by the painter Dora Carrington. The windows overlook a quiet English garden. There's a small round table where Woolf and other members of the Bloomsbury group sat and argued and crafted their positions and published their thoughts. One can see why that environment might induce Woolf's yearning for a similar space of her own, for the safe space men reserved for men in that society: for not just a room but *the room* to think.

It's peaceful, the Rylands Suite, and I sat in every chair at that little round table in order to maximize the chances of sitting where Woolf might have sat; and I wrote as much as I possibly could in the week I had to enjoy it.

Of course, there is quite an old-fashioned sense of effete leisureliness in this yearning. It is increasingly rare, to find that privileged, unstressed, low-tech way of being educated and of conducting interpersonal exchange.

But I cite this experience because it's not a bad thing to sit and talk, face to face, to argue in close quarters while sharing a meal. As a starting point for political exchange, it just seems a better ideal of free speech than the display of big guns as the pinnacle of expressive freedom. Acknowledging a legal right bounded only by harassment or intimidation doesn't seem to get us far.

This contrast is one worth exploring: so let me take the quaint rose-scented scenario of the Rylands Suite and place it next to another story about how we structure the room we have to speak: Some years ago, I was visiting Nottingham, England, when the evangelical minister Terry Jones and the Dove World Outreach Center of Gainesville, Florida, burst onto the global media stage by soaking a Koran in kerosene and setting it aflame. This occurred after he'd conducted a so-called mock 'trial' of Islam for being 'of the Devil'. The Koran was 'found guilty and a copy was burned'. With hubristic conflation of his church and our state – as well as of magic and legality – Jones proclaimed, 'The court system of America does not allow convicted criminals to go free. And that is why we feel obligated to do this.'[4]

Pastor Jones had a congregation of no more than fifty followers. But Pastor Jones also felt obligated to broadcast the incineration online. As his deeds flashed around the globe, they were mirrored in fundamentalist kind, particularly in Afghanistan, where an American drone had recently killed a group of children and, separately, twelve American soldiers were pending trial for the 'sport' killing of random civilians – behaviour that included mutilation, dismemberment and the retention of body parts as souvenirs. Riots broke out, and in the city of Mazar-i-Sharif, the local UN compound became the object of outrage. Twelve staff were killed.

At the same time as Pastor Jones was engaged in burning the Koran in Florida, I was ensconced on the edge of Sherwood Forest, sipping a beer at the oldest pub in

Britain, 'Ye Olde Trip to Jerusalem'. It purportedly dates to 1189, the year Richard the Lionheart was crowned and then joined the Third Crusade. The pub was supposedly a hangout for soldiers who gathered before their quest to retake the Holy Land from Muslim 'infidels'. The Third Crusade, like those before and after, resulted in a bloodbath. The siege of the city of Acre alone led to the slaughter of nearly 3,000 Muslim captives, many of whom were said to have been disembowelled in search of swallowed gemstones.[5] This was also the period during which the Hashshashin – from which the word 'assassin' is derived – refined the arts of sabotage and infiltration. The Hashshashin, a small, secretive cult of Persian warriors, conducted their own brand of unconventional, self-interested warfare against ruling Muslim caliphates as well as invading crusaders.[6] Much like Al Qaeda today, they played both sides against the middle, often murdering for hire.

So there I perched, on a sandstone cliff in England's fair Midlands, my feet planted in the Middle Ages, my iBrain iPadded with tweets about Pastor Jones. As it turned out, Pastor Jones (perhaps not coincidentally a high school classmate of Rush Limbaugh[7]) had been personally and publicly begged not to pursue what he dubbed 'International Burn a Koran Day' by no less than General David Petraeus, Secretary of State Hillary Clinton, Secretary of Defense Daryl Gates, President

Barack Obama and even Sarah Palin. To no avail: Jones – like the Westboro Baptist Church, with which his Dove Center sometimes joined league – pressed on unhindered by compassion or the courts.

When the Dove World Outreach Center broadcast its burning of the Koran online, it tapped into the unprecedented technological ability to link radically narrow worldviews in a fashion so sudden, so powerful and so complete that it was almost like atoms smashing. Pastor Jones deployed language in an unyieldingly fundamentalist way: words were rendered incarnate, as though utterance were embodied – the word alive, amplified, globally incendiary.

Much like discussions about mass shooters who cite President Trump as inspiration, it is hard to say that Jones 'caused' the deaths in the UN compound in Afghanistan. Indeed, Jones issued a statement expressing his sorrow at the deaths in Mazar-i-Sharif, while denying any responsibility and calling for retribution.[8]

As a headline in the *Christian Science Monitor* put it: 'If Terry Jones burns the Koran, he'll also set fire to America's identity.'[9] Just so, Jones repeatedly described the Koran as though it were a golem, a real defendant embodying all of Islam. And for their part, Afghan mullahs and their inspired mobs saw Jones as the reified homunculus of institutional American force. Indeed, they burned both Jones and President Obama in effigy.[10]

The conceptual artist Sol LeWitt once observed that 'the idea becomes a machine that makes the art'.[11] President Trump has fired up a machine that independently regenerates this behaviour, so reminiscent of the Crusades. I cannot help thinking of a tweet sent by President Trump's son, Donald Jr, on January 4, 2020, the day after his father had assassinated Qasem Soleimani, head of Iran's Quds Force. In the image, Donald Jr. was holding up to the viewer an enormous assault rifle – a special edition called 'The Crusader' – with a Celtic Cross forged on the barrel and a cartoon of an imprisoned Hillary Clinton affixed to the magazine.[12] For all our rationalist inclinations, thoughts really do perform sometimes as animations. The heated familiarity of old battle cries is given new force by technology.

IX. *The First Lady of the Land*

'I've always had a weakness for lost causes once they're really lost.'[1]

In December 2016, the then President-elect Donald Trump went to Mobile, Alabama, as part of a victory tour. His welcome at the airport was quite the show: the then Senator Jeff Sessions met him on the tarmac amid a flotilla of teenaged girls attired in full antebellum ballroom regalia – frou-frou gowns in Easter egg colours, with hoop skirts and large frilled hats. They were the Azalea Trail Maids, local high school seniors chosen every year since 1951 to act as 'ambassadors' for the city of Mobile. It is considered an honour to be selected, and it would not be unfair to suppose that the wedding-cake frippery is meant to suggest the flower of Southern girlhood, the romance of debutante cotillions, the languidness of steamboats on the Mississippi and the plantation politics of *Gone with the Wind*, as well as impenetrably layered maidenhood.

On close inspection of the scene, which was splashed across the front pages of most major American newspapers at the time, one could see that at least one of the maids, smiling shyly from beneath the shade of a lavender sun bonnet, was Black. I was startled by a figure that immediately brought to mind a twinning doll – a common nineteenth-century toy with two heads, whose torsos met in the middle, with a long skirt. Held vertically, the skirt would fall and obscure the other end: flipped one way, it became a white doll; turned the other, a black doll was revealed. As scholar Robin Bernstein has observed, the 'fusion of black and white referred to racial mixing, sex and rape in the plantation system. African American women, the most likely creators of this doll form stitched politically volatile ideas into the children's toy and thereby made these ideas appear innocent.'[2] Here, it was as though one doll had been accidentally on purpose turned upside down. Most of Mobile's city officials defended the costumes – as well as the gender politics – as representing the new, integrated Alabama.

It was an interesting gesture – to take an iconic image of white womanhood and insert a brown face or two – but if the aim was to 'fix' the old and project the new, it failed. Instead of speaking to the question of present-day equality for Black women or girls, it sought to enfold them in revisionist ideologies. To me, the great-great-granddaughter of the offspring-made-property of plantation masters, the literal attempt to dress up historical atrocity is painful; when those gowns were in fashion, Black girls were owned, bestialized and impregnated for profit. Here was a project that, first, sanitized history by resurrecting the dead from all sides of a conflict and, second, draped them in costumes representing the more morally indefensible side – with the implicit caption 'See how far we've come!' This was Confederate sentimentality disguised as colour-blindness.

'Isn't inclusion what you wanted?' 'You're the one debasing this happy cotillion with foul intention!' Such discourse is often deployed to displace responsibility for racial distrust: there is talk of Blacks 'playing the race card', or defensive posturing whereby white attempts to accommodate Black people are deemed proleptically futile, and sure to be met with ingratitude. Robin Bernstein describes romanticizing of this sort of framing as 'not only the ability to remember while appearing to forget, but even more powerfully, the production of racial memory through the performance of forgetting'. What choices for self-figuration does this circular folly suggest to Black girls and women? A conventionally 'pretty' picture captures the spirit of a whole system predicated on certain figures being ornamental, spoken for and styled, for better or for worse, by others. In her book, *The Law Is a White Dog: How legal rituals make and unmake persons*, the anthropologist Colin Dayan describes the 'afterlife of ostracism' as 'disposability', or the phenomenon of 'incessantly dying in new ways'.[3] It is an elegant way of tracing the bottom line: how does anyone survive having been marked with the trope of un-life? Is there a path to vivacity from being captured and captioned as the object of others' beliefs?

Racialized wall-building has terrible and irrational consequences for us all. It lends authority to forms of segregation whose paths unfurl towards extinction. The casting of curses settles into the bones, a coiled power ready to strike when suddenly unsettled, no longer a joke, no longer a spot of bad judgement, no longer laughable at all.

> She stood for a moment remembering the small things, the avenue of dark cedars leading to Tara, the banks of cape jessamine bushes, vivid green against the white walls, the fluttering white curtains. And Mammy would be there. Suddenly she wanted Mammy desperately, as she had wanted her when she was a little girl, wanted the broad bosom on which to lay her head, the gnarled black hand on her hair. Mammy, the last link with the old days.[4]

Notes

I. *'The Battle of Love'*

1. Margaret Mitchell, *Gone with the Wind*. New York: The Macmillan Company, 1936. Reprint, New York: Macmillan, 1957. Citations refer to the 1957 edition. Hereafter referred to as *GWTW*.
2. Jean Baudrillard, *The Transparency of Evil: Essays on Extreme Phenomena*, translation by James Benedict. London: Verso, 1993. p. 7.
3. W. E. B. Du Bois, *The Souls of Black Folk*. Chicago: A. C. McClurg & Co., 1903.
4. Michael Kimmelman, 'Charleston Needs That African American Museum. And Now', *The New York Times*, March 29, 2018.
5. Thomas Dixon, *The Clansman: An Historical Romance of the Ku Klux Klan*. New York: Doubleday, Page & Co., 1905.
6. *Ibid.*, p. 67.
7. *Ibid.*, p. 149.
8. Laura Isensee, 'Why Calling Slaves "Workers" Is More Than An Editing Error', National Public Radio, October 23, 2015; see also, Margaret Biser, 'I used to lead tours at a plantation. You won't believe the questions I got about slavery', *Vox*, August 28, 2017.
9. Gillian Brockell, 'Some white people don't want to hear about slavery at plantations built by slaves', *Washington Post*, August 8, 2019.
10. *GWTW*, p. 54.

11. *Ibid*.
12. *Ibid*., pp. 17–18. Quotation from Pat Conroy's Preface to the Scribner edition of *Gone with the Wind* (New York: Scribner, 2011). All subsequent citations from Pat Conroy's Preface refer to the 2011 Scribner edition.
13. *Ibid*., p. 678.
14. Thomas Jefferson, *Notes on the State of Virginia*, 1785.
15. Frances Anne Kemble, *Journal of a Residence on a Georgian Plantation in 1838–1839*. Georgia: Brown Thrasher Books, 1863. Reprint, Georgia: University of Georgia Press, 1984.
16. See, 'The 1927 Slave Auction at Monticello', https://www.monticello.org/slaveauction/
17. 'Recollections of Peter Fossett', *The New York World*, January 30, 1898.
18. Frederick Douglass, *Narrative of the Life of Frederick Douglass, an American Slave*, London: H. G. Collins, 1851, p. 45.
19. James Baldwin, 'The White Man's Guilt', in *Baldwin: Collected Essays*. New York: Library of America, 1998. p. 723.
20. Laura Vozella and Gregory Schneider, 'Gov. Northam refuses to step down, despite flood of calls for his resignation over racist photo', *Washington Post*, February 2, 2019.
21. Adeel Hassan, 'Virginia's First Lady Apologizes for Handing Cotton to Black Students on Tour', *The New York Times*, February 28, 2019.
22. 'Kevin Beasley's Raw Materials', *Art 21*, February 6, 2019.
23. 'Virginia Gov. Ralph Northam Draws Scorn for "Indentured Servants" Remark', *The Daily Beast*, February 10, 2019.
24. Ethan Kytle and Blain Roberts, *Denmark Vesey's Garden: Slavery and Memory in the Cradle of the Confederacy*. New York: The New Press, 2018. p. 170.
25. *GWTW*, pp. 679–680.
26. Peter Sblendorio, 'Sportscaster Warner Wolf arrested for taking the word "Plantation" off sign at his gated community', *New York Daily News*, February 8, 2019.

27. Teo Armus, 'St. Louis lawyer who waved gun at protesters says he was "victim of a mob"', *Washington Post*, July 1, 2020.
28. Walter Johnson, 'The Revolution at the Gate', *Boston Review*, July 7, 2020.
29. *Ibid.*
30. Teo Armus, 'St. Louis lawyer who waved gun at protesters says he was "victim of a mob"', the *Washington Post*, July 1, 2020.
31. 'Central West End couple explains why they pointed guns at protesters who demanded Krewson's resignation', *KMOV4 News*, June 29, 2020.
32. *GWTW*, p. 439.
33. Donald Trump has claimed that there are seventy-seven walls worldwide, researchers say that 'seven such barriers are not expected to materialise any time soon and are still in the planning stage' as of 2019. Palko Karasz, 'Fact Check: Trump's Tweet on Border Walls in Europe', *The New York Times*, January 17, 2019.
34. Nadja Sayej, 'Ai Weiwei launches controversial public art project focused on immigration', *Guardian*, October 17, 2017.
35. Jessica Kutz, 'Triumph and tragedy: Trump's border wall expands', *High Country News*, April 20, 2020.
36. Gus Bova, 'Audio: Border Patrol Plans to Light Up Butterfly Refuge Like a "War Zone"', *Texas Observer*, January 16, 2019.
37. *I Never Saw Another Butterfly: Children's Drawings and Poems from Terezin Concentration Camp 1942–1944*, edited by Hana Volavkova. New York: Schocken Press, 1994.
38. Josh Begley, 'Prison Map', http://prisonmap.com/
39. Nicholas Mirzeoff, 'Ghostwriting: working out visual culture', *Journal of Visual Culture*, vol. 1(2): 239–254, 2002.
40. Nicholas Mirzeoff, *The Right to Look: A Counterhistory of Visuality*, Duke University Press, 2011.

II. 'The Supreme Test'

1. *GWTW*, p. 651.
2. *GWTW*, p. 16.
3. Chiara Bottici and Benoit Challand, *The Politics of Imagination*, Birkbeck Law Press, 2011, p. 3.
4. *GWTW*, p. 18.
5. Thomas Dixon, *The Clansman: An Historical Romance of the Ku Klux Klan*. New York: Doubleday, Page & Co., 1905. p. i.
6. *Ibid.*, p. 74.
7. Helen Klein Ross, 'Hatred Endorsed by a President', *Lapham's Quarterly*, November 8, 2018.
8. Alex Horton, 'A Latina novelist spoke about white privilege. Students burned her book in response', *Washington Post*, October 11, 2019.
9. The white students who burned the book seemed to be saying that Crucet had dumped on all white people when she mentioned the flow of white tears. In this instance, however, it might appear that 'white tears' and 'white privilege' were displaced by an intense and seemingly contagious 'white rage' at being asked to look around and interrogate where all the people of colour might be.
10. 'Tucson's Mexican-American Studies Ban', *The Daily Show with Jon Stewart*', April 2, 2012; see also, Rebecca Huval, 'Updates from the Tucson Unified School District', *Independent Lens Newsletter*, Public Broadcasting Corporation, April 18, 2012.
11. *Ibid*.
12. 'Federal judge tells Arizona it can't ban Mexican American studies', *Washington Post*, December 28, 2017.
13. Diana Dillaber Murray, '"Teacher of the Year" alleges she was fired from Pontiac school over Trayvon Martin fundraiser', *Daily Tribune*, April 10, 2012.
14. Naomi Schaefer Riley, 'The Most Persuasive Case For Eliminating Black Studies? Just Read the Dissertations', *The Chronicle of Higher Education Blog*, May, 2012.

15. *Ibid.*; see also, *The Nation*, June 4, 2012; and Gene Demby, 'Naomi Schaefer Riley, Chronicle of Higher Education Blogger, Fired For Calling Black Studies "Claptrap"', *Huffington Post*, May 8, 2012.

III. 'Across the Chasm'

1. *GWTW*, p. 435.
2. Frederick Douglass, *Narrative of the Life of Frederick Douglass, an American Slave*, p. 23.
3. Amber Phillips, '"They're rapists." President Trump's campaign launch speech two years later, annotated', *Washington Post*, June 16, 2017; see also, Jessica Kwong, 'Donald Trump Suggests "Very Bad" People, Gangs and Drug Dealers in Bahamas Could Be Trying to Enter U.S.', *Newsweek*, September 9, 2019.
4. Chauncey DeVega, 'Donald Trump's war on the poor has historical precedent – and it's not pretty', Salon.com, March 20, 2017.
5. Brandon Soderberg and Baynard Woods, 'Think Federal Cops in Portland are Scary? Cops Use "Jump-Out Boys2" All the Time', *Guardian*, July 29, 2020.
6. Maegan Vazquez, 'Trump circulates quote invoking "civil war-like fracture" if he's removed from office', CNN Politics, September 30, 2019.
7. Ivan Pereira, 'Thousands of armed protesters turn out for Trump-supported gun rally', *ABC News*, January 20, 2020.
8. Lee Moran, 'Donald Trump Torched Over "Gone with the Wind" Lament: "The Doggiest Dogwhistle"', *Huffington Post*, February 21, 2020.
9. Stuart Oldham, 'Ben Affleck Apologizes for PBS Slavery Censorship: "I Was Embarrassed"', *Variety*, April 21, 2015.
10. Alondra Nelson, *The Social Life of DNA: Race, Reparations and Reconciliation after the Genome*, Beacon Press, 2016.

11. 'To Infinity and Beyond!' is Buzz Lightyear's famous catchphrase in the Pixar *Toy Story* films and the TV series *Buzz Lightyear of Star Command*.

IV. 'The Snare of the Fowler'

1. *GWTW*, p. 197.
2. From 'Home' by Warsan Shire, 2014.
3. 'Deported Parents May Lose Their Kids To Adoption', The Associated Press, NBC News, October 9, 2018.
4. Nomaan Merchant, 'Judge: US must free migrant children from family detention', *Washington Post*, June 26, 2020.
5. Spencer Hsu, 'US might separate families after federal judge orders ICE to free migrant children', *Washington Post*, July 7, 2020.
6. Frederick Douglass, *Narrative of the Life of Frederick Douglass, an American Slave*, p. 12.
7. Richard R. W. Brooks and Carol M. Rose, *Saving the Neighborhood: Racially Restrictive Covenants, Law, and Social Norms*, Harvard University Press, 2013.
8. Keeanga-Yamahtta Taylor, *Race for Profit: How Banks and the Real Estate Industry Undermined Black Home Ownership*, University of North Carolina Press, 2019.
9. Robin DiAngelo, *White Fragility: Why It's So Hard for White People To Talk About Racism*, Beacon Press, 2018.
10. Tim Wise, *White Like Me: Reflections on Race from a Privileged Son*, Soft Skull Press, 2011.

V. 'The Eyes of the Jungle'

1. *GWTW*, from Sidney Howard's screenplay.
2. Vivek Saxena, '"Blue Flu" hits terrified city: Atlanta cops refuse to work after DA charges officer with felony murder', *Business and Politics Review*, June 18, 2020; Stephen Crockett, Jr., 'Police Officers Refuse to Work LA

High School After Players Kneel During National Anthem',
The Root, September 28, 2016; Jamelle Bouie, 'Criminal
Neglect: By refusing to police the streets, Baltimore's cops
are fueling the city's lawlessness and violence', Slate.com,
June 18, 2015.

3. 'Trump says NFL should fire players who kneel during
   national anthem', *Los Angeles Times*, September 22,
   2017.

4. 'H.R. 3162 – Uniting and Strengthening America by
   Providing Appropriate Tools Required to Intercept and
   Obstruct Terrorism (USA Patriot Act) Act of 2001.'

5. Emma Graham Harrison, '"Enemy of the people":
   Trump's phrase and its echoes of totalitarianism',
   Guardian, August 3, 2018.

6. The reporter Jim Acosta of CNN was banned from the
   White House for asking 'nasty' questions in November
   2018, although he later successfully sued to reinstate his
   press pass. Other journalists banned from certain White
   House briefings include: Kaitlan Collins of CNN, Jonathan
   Lemire of The Associated Press, Jeff Mason of Reuters,
   Justin Sink from Bloomberg and Eli Stokols of the *Los
   Angeles Times*.

7. Tamara Keith, 'President Trump's Description of What's
   "Fake" Is Expanding', National Public Radio, September 2,
   2018.

8. For now, I am not foregrounding certain intentional and
   complex forms of head-butting, where political action
   committees or 'dark money' or special interest
   organizations pay to sow discord or to 'out' people or to
   film campus encounters for the sole purpose of mocking
   them on widely dispersed social media. This is a problem
   of technological *dispositifs*, distorting face-to-face
   encounters and making them a game of entrapment and
   shaming, an industry akin to revenge porn, the
   manufacture of outrage. It's definitely a problem, but
   mostly beyond my scope for purposes of this essay. For

now, I simply wish to caution against the too-easy assumption that 'words will never hurt us'. Words can and do just that.

9. Jeff Muskus, 'Sarah Palin's PAC Puts Gun Sights On Democrats She's Targeting in 2010', *Huffington Post*, January 9, 2011.

10. Russ Chastain, 'Good Guys With Guns Are the Best Defense', *All Outdoor*, January 3, 2020; see also, Meghan Keneally, 'Breaking down the NRA-backed theory that a good guy with a gun stops a bad guy with a gun', *ABC News*, October 29, 2018.

11. *District of Columbia v. Heller*, 554 U.S. 570 (2008); see also, *McDonald v. City of Chicago*, 561 U.S. 742 (2010).

12. S.B. No.11, 'An Act', Texas Government Code Section 411.2031.

13. Penal Code, Title 9. Offenses Against Public Order and Decency, Chapter 43. Public Indecency.

14. Tom Dart, 'Cocks Not Glocks: Texas students carry dildos on campus to protest gun law', *Guardian*, August 25, 2016.

15. For example, 'Frat bans 13 Who Wore Blackface', *Los Angeles Times*, November 9, 2001; 'Fraternity brothers posed in blackface and gangster costumes, this college's latest racist dust-up', *Washington Post*, April 10, 2018; Cleve Woodson, Jr., 'The lengthy history of white politicians wearing blackface – and getting a pass', *Washington Post*, February 16, 2019.

16. Leyland Cecco, 'Trudeau says he can't recall how many times he wore blackface makeup', *Guardian*, September 20, 2019.

17. Morwenna Ferrier, 'Gucci withdraws $890 jumper after blackface backlash', *Guardian*, February 7, 2019.

18. Jason Dike, 'Moncler Steps into Controversy with Collection Inspired by Racist Dolls', Highsnobiety, July 15, 2016.

19. 'Prada pulls figurines that resembled blackface from New York store', *Guardian*, December 15, 2018.

20. Caitlin Yilek, 'Another one: Virginia AG Mark Herring admits to wearing blackface in 1980', *Washington Examiner*, February 6, 2019.
21. 'SEE IT: Covington Catholic High students in blackface at past basketball game', *New York Daily News*, January 21, 2019.
22. Robin Givhan, 'Blackface is white supremacy as fashion – and it's always been in season', *Washington Post*, February 7, 2019.
23. *Ibid.*
24. Olivia Messer, 'Covington Catholic Teen on "Fox & Friends": Blackface is "School Sprit"': *The Daily Beast*, January 23, 2019.
25. Robin Givhan, 'Blackface is white supremacy as fashion – and it's always been in season', *Washington Post*, February 7, 2019.

VI. *'The Great Heart'*

1. *GWTW*, p. 1006.
2. Mary Douglas, *Purity and Danger*, Routledge Classics, 2002.
3. Isabel Wilkerson, *Caste: The Origin of Our Discontents*, Random House, 2020.
4. Seung Min Kim, 'Trump decries migrant children: "They're not innocent"', *The Mercury News*, May 23, 2018.
5. Gregory Korte and Alan Gomez, 'Trump ramps up rhetoric on undocumented immigrants: "These aren't people. These are animals"', *USA Today*, May 16, 2018.
6. *Ibid.*
7. 'Transcript: White House Chief of Staff John Kelly's Interview with NPR', National Public Radio, May 11, 2018; see also, Amy Davidson Sorkin, 'The Case of the Missing Immigrant Children', *The New Yorker*, May 29, 2018.
8. Bill Hutchinson, 'More than 30,000 children under age 10 have been arrested in the US since 2013: FBI', *ABC News*, October 1, 2019.

9. 'Detention of Child Migrants at the U.S. Border Surges to Record Levels', *The New York Times*, October 29, 2019.

10. 'How many migrant children are detained in US custody?', *Guardian*, December 22, 2018.

11. Julia Ainsley, 'Thousands more migrant kids separated from parents under Trump than previously reported', NBC News, January 17, 2019.

12. Michael Miller, Emma Brown and Aaron Davis, 'Inside Casa Padre, the converted Walmart where the U.S. is holding nearly 1,500 immigrant children', *Washington Post*, June 14, 2018.

13. Emily McFarlan Miller and Yonat Shimron, 'Why is Jeff Sessions quoting Romans 13 and why is the bible verse so often invoked?', *USA Today*, June 16, 2018.

14. 'Eugenics Record Office', Archives at Cold Spring Harbor Laboratory; Andrea DenHoed, 'The Forgotten Lessons of the American Eugenics Movement', *The New Yorker*, April 27, 2016.

15. Molly Ladd Taylor, *Fixing The Poor*, Johns Hopkins Press, 2018.

16. Scott W. Stern, *The Trials of Nina McCall*, Beacon Press, 2018.

17. Shatema Threadcraft, *Intimate Justice: The Black Female Body and the Body Politic*, Oxford University Press, 2016.

18. Susan Schweik, *The Ugly Laws: Disability in Public*, New York University Press, 2008.

19. Mariel Padilla, 'Orlando Officer is Terminated After Arresting 6-Year-Olds', *The New York Times*, September 23, 2019; see also 'Update 1-U.S. sues Mississippi officials over student arrests', *Chicago Tribune*, October 24, 2012.

20. Michelle Alexander, *The New Jim Crow: Mass Incarceration in the Age of Colorblindness*, The New Press, 2012.

21. Tim Giago, *Children Left Behind: The Dark Legacy of Indian Mission Boarding Schools*, Clear Light Publishing, 2006; David Wallace Adams, *Education for Extinction: American Indians and the Boarding School Experience, 1875–1928*,

University of Kansas Press, 1995; *American Indian Boarding Schools: An Exploration of Global Ethnic & Cultural Cleaning*, The Ziibiwing Center of Anishinabe Culture and Lifeways, 2011; Roxanne Dunbar-Ortiz, *An Indigenous Peoples' History of the United States*, Beacon Press, 2015.

22. Matthew Haag, 'Thousands of Immigrant Children Said They Were Sexually Abused in U.S. Detention Centers, Report Says', *The New York Times*, February 27, 2019.

23. Eli Rosenberg, 'Ann Coulter tells Trump that immigrant children are "child actors", in Fox News interview', *Independent*, June 19, 2018.

24. Madeline Hsu, *The Good Immigrants: How the Yellow Peril Became the Model Minority*, Princeton University Press, 2018.

25. Michi Weglyn, *Years of Infamy: The untold story of America's concentration camps*, Morrow Publishing, 1976.

26. Michelle Alexander, *The New Jim Crow: Mass Incarceration in the Age of Colorblindness*, The New Press, 2012.

27. Dylan Stableford, 'Donald Trump on ISIS: "You have to take out their families"', *Yahoo News*, December 2, 2015.

28. Yoka Verdoner, 'Nazis separated me from my parents as a child. The trauma lasts a lifetime', *Guardian*, June 18, 2018; see also, Richard Lukas, *Did the Children Cry? Hitler's War against Jewish and Polish Children*, Hippocrene Books, 2001.

29. Shalita O'Neal, 'Foster Care and Homelessness', *Foster Focus Magazine*, vol. 5, issue 3, August, 2015.

30. Laura Bauer and Judy L. Thomas, 'Throwaway Kids: We are sending more foster kids to prison than college', *The Kansas City Star*, December 15, 2019.

31. 'Conditions in Migrant Detention Centers', *American Oversight*, July 7, 2020.

32. Chris Cillizza, 'Melania Trump totally changed her story on the "I really don't care" jacket', CNN Politics, October 14, 2018.

33. 'When a Jacket Isn't Just a Jacket – The Fascist Message of "I Don't Care"', *The Daily Kos*, June 25, 2018.
34. Tobias Jones, 'The fascist movement that has brought Mussolini back to the mainstream', *Guardian*, February 22, 2018.
35. Bethania Palma, 'Is Melania Trump Fluent in Five Languages?', *Snopes*, December 30, 2019.
36. Jon Stone, 'Slovenian right-wingers try to form government and oust liberals after election gains', the *Independent*, June 4, 2018; see also, 'Feature: Slovenia Gets New Far-Right Party, the "Homeland League"', *Total Slovenia News*, March 19, 2019.

VII. 'Vengeance Is Mine'

1. GWTW, p. 652.
2. Susan Svrluga, 'Trump signs executive order on free speech on college campuses', *Washington Post*, March 21, 2019.
3. Justin Wise, 'Trump suggests that it could get "very bad" if military, police, biker supporters play "tough"', *The Hill*, March 14, 2019.
4. Mary Beth Sheridan and Mariana Zuniga, 'Maduro's muscle: Politically backed motorcycle gangs known as "collectivos" are the enforcers for Venezuela's authoritarian leader', *Washington Post*, March 14, 2019.
5. Dolna Krupa, 'The Night Wolves, Putin's biker gang', *The Economist*, August 23, 2018.
6. Reis Thebault, 'Steve King posts meme warning that red states have "8trillion bullets" in event of civil war', *Washington Post*, March 19, 2019.
7. Jonathan Lemire, 'Trump downplays white nationalism threat after massacre', Fox News, March 16, 2019.
8. Aaron Rupar, 'Kellyanne Conway's stunningly irresponsible advice: read New Zealander mosque shooter's manifesto', *Vox*, March 18, 2019.

9. Adolf Hitler, *Mein Kampf*, Houghton Mifflin, 1943.
10. Abigail Simon, 'People Are Angry President Trump Used This Word to Describe Undocumented Immigrants', *Time Magazine*, June 19, 2019; see also, Michael Harriot, 'All the Times Donald Trump Tweeted the Word "Infested"', *The Root*, July 29, 2019.
11. Ayal Feinberg, Regina Branton and Valerie Martinez-Ebers, 'Counties that hosted a 2016 Trump rally saw a 226 percent increase in hate crimes', *Washington Post*, March 22, 2019; see also, Louis Jacobson, 'Did counties hosting a Trump rally in 2016 see a 226% spike in hate crimes?', *Politifact*, The Poynter Institute, August 12, 2019.
12. Jamie Ross, 'Liam Neeson Says He Went Out Hoping to Kill a "Black Bastard" after Someone Close to Him Was Raped', *The Daily Beast*, February 4, 2019.
13. Clemence Michallon, 'Liam Neeson interview: Rape, race and how I learnt revenge doesn't work', *Independent*, February 4, 2019.
14. Donald Bogle, *Toms, Coons, Mulattoes, Mammies and Bucks: An Interpretive History of Blacks in American Films*, Bloomsbury Academic, 5th edition, 2016.
15. Melvin Patrick Ely, *The Adventures of Amos 'n' Andy: A Social History of an American Phenomenon*, The Free Press, 1991.
16. Hannah Al-Othman, 'Not how old were they? How tall were they? You just asked what color were they? I don't care how sorry you are, Liam Neeson, that is disgusting.' Tweet, @HannahAlOthman, February 4, 2019.
17. Claudia Rankine, *Citizen: An American Lyric*, Greywolf Press, 2014, p. 63.
18. Lynne Tirrell, 'Genocidal Language Games', in Maitra and McGowan (eds.), *Speech and Harm: Controversies Over Free Speech*, Oxford University Press, 2012, pp. 174–221; see also, Lynne Tirrell, 'Toxic Speech: Toward an Epidemiology of Discursive Harm', *Philosophical Topics*, vol. 45, no. 2, 139–161, 2017.

19. *Ibid*.
20. *Ibid*.
21. Jose Del Real, '"Get 'em out!" Racial tensions explode at Donald Trump's rallies', the *Washington Post*, March 12, 2016.
22. Michael E. Miller, 'Donald Trump on a protester: "I'd like to punch him in the face"', *Washington Post*, February 23, 2016.
23. Melissa Chan, 'Trump May Pay Legal Fees of Man Who Sucker-Punched Protester', *Time Magazine*, March 13, 2016.
24. Adolf Hitler, *Mein Kampf*, Houghton Mifflin, 1943, pp. 478–479.

VIII. 'The Fiery Cross'

1. *GWTW*, p. 928.
2. T. J. Cribb, 'Obituary: George Rylands', *Independent*, January 20, 1999.
3. Virginia Woolf, *A Room of One's Own*, Hogarth Press, 1929.
4. Lizette Alvarez and Don Van Natta, Jr., 'Pastor Who Burned Koran Demands Retribution', *The New York Times*, April 1, 2011.
5. John D. Hosler, *The Seige of Acre, 1189–1191: Saladin, Richard the Lionheart, and the Battle That Decided the Third Crusade*, Yale University Press, 2018.
6. Bernard Lewis, *The Assassins*, Weidenfeld & Nicolson, 1967.
7. Emi Kolawole, 'Rush Limbaugh and Terry Jones were high school classmates', the *Washington Post*, September 10, 2010.
8. Aliyah Shahid, 'Pastor Terry Jones on deadly Afghanistan protests at United Nations compound: Don't blame me!', *New York Daily News*, April 2, 2011.
9. Seeme Hasan and Mansoor Ijaz, 'Commentary: If Terry Jones burns the Koran, he'll also set fire to America's identity', *Christian Science Monitor*, September 9, 2010.

10. Katie Nelson, 'Muslims burn effigy of Obama in Afghanistan; President Karzai demands pastor Terry Jones be punished', *New York Daily News*, April 3, 2011.
11. Sol LeWitt, 'Paragraphs on Conceptual Art', in *Art Forum International*, Summer, 1967; reprinted in *SFAQ: International Art and Culture* as 'Sol LeWitt on Conceptual Art – 1967', November 29, 2011.
12. Sarah Pulliam Bailey, 'Donald Trump, Jr. poses with rifle decorated with a cross used during the Crusades', *Washington Post*, January 6, 2020. This image is in disturbing counterpoint to conceptual artist Mel Chin's 2002 rendering of a Celtic Cross, welded and shaped from a group of AK-47 assault rifles. Chin calls the piece 'Cross for the Unforgiven'.

IX. *'The First Lady of the Land'*

1. GWTW, from Sidney Howard's screenplay.
2. Robin Bernstein, *Racial Innocence: Performing American childhood from slavery to civil rights*, New York University Press, 2011, p. 20.
3. Colin Dayan, *The Law Is a White Dog: How legal rituals make and unmake persons*, Princeton University Press, 2011.
4. *GWTW*, p. 1042.

Acknowledgements

I wish to thank my remarkable editors at the *Times Literary Supplement*, Rozalind Dineen and Thea Lenarduzzi. I am indebted to them for suggesting I write this book to begin with, and for their subsequent encouragement, patience and very careful reads.

I am also indebted to Joseph Spadafore, editor of Volume 64 of the *McGill Law Journal*. It was he, along with the editorial board, who invited me to give their annual lecture, on 'the role of a neighbor and how ideas travel'. I presented that lecture in 2018, but subsequently a messy patch of life got in the way. To my enduring regret, I did not finish the accompanying article in time for publication in the *Journal*. But that richly provocative invitation was the seed from which this book grew.

I finally did return to this project and get it done thanks to the gentle but persistent urging of Julia Mendoza, who served as my tireless and incomparably brilliant teaching assistant while completing her doctoral studies. Julia was kind enough to devote endless hours discussing ideas, examining drafts and giving me feedback on every iteration of this essay. Her intelligence, humour, patience and generosity have been utterly indispensable resources throughout this process.

I also wish to thank the other friends and colleagues whose thoughts informed my own along the way: Atossa Abrahamian, Josh Begley, Robin Bernstein, Richard Blint, Margaret Burnham, Eduardo Cadava, Cynthia Dwork, Elizabeth Emens, Patricia Ewick, Daniela Gandorfer, Nancy Goldstein, Michele Goodwin, Don Guttenplan, James Hackney, Alice Hearst, Joseph Lawless, Sarah Leonard, Caroline Light, Jane Lipson, Bradley McCallum, Martha Minow, Marya Pollack, Robert Pollack, Alain Rogier, Marcia Sells, Susan Silbey, Constance St. Louis, Ann Stoler, Martha Umphrey, Katrina Vanden Heuvel, and Peter Williams.

Finally, I wish to express my deep gratitude to the institutions whose funding and support underwrote this project: the Carl and Lily Pforzheimer Foundation, Columbia University School of Law, the Institute for Critical Social Inquiry at The New School, Kent University Summer School on Critical Theory, *The Nation*, The Nation Institute, Northeastern University Department of Philosophy and Religion, Northeastern University School of Law, The Radcliffe Institute for Advanced Study, and the Schlesinger Library for Women's History.